PHEASANT SHOOTING

Other books by David Hudson published by Swan Hill Press

Running Your Own Shoot
The Working Labrador
The Small Shoot
Working Pointers and Setters

PHEASANT SHOOTING

David Hudson

SWAN·HILL
PRESS

Copyright © 2005 David Hudson

First published in the UK in 2005
by Swan Hill Press, an imprint of Quiller Publishing Ltd

British Library Cataloguing-in-Publication Data
A catalogue record for this book
is available from the British Library

ISBN 1 904057 59 4

Printed in China

Swan Hill Press

An imprint of Quiller Publishing Ltd
Wykey House, Wykey, Shrewsbury, SY4 1JA
Tel: 01939 261616 Fax: 01939 261606
E-mail: info@quillerbooks.com
Website: www.swanhillbooks.com

CONTENTS

Pheasant shooting needs beaters and dogs as well as guns.

1

INTRODUCTION

I shot my first pheasant as it rose, cackling, from a field of Brussels sprouts during the freezing winter of 1963. I was using a single-barrelled twelve-bore shotgun made by Harrington and Richardson that I had salvaged from a garden shed. It had required liberal applications of penetrating oil and elbow grease to remove the accumulated rust from years of neglect though there was little I could do to disguise the woodworm holes in the stock. Nevertheless, I was as proud of that gun as if it had been a Purdey or a Boss. I seem to remember paying the previous owner £1 for the gun which was probably a fair estimate of its value.

I was mooching through the sprout field with three lads from the neighbouring village, ostensibly in pursuit of pigeons. It was a bright, sunny and bitterly cold day with a deep blanket of snow covering the frozen ground. The pheasant got up: someone dared me to shoot it: the gun came up and went Bang! and the pheasant...

It would be nice to report that it crumpled and fell, cleanly killed by a single shot. What actually happened was that it shed a few feathers and flew on straight towards the farm at Wood Hall, then towered high into the sky before falling, stone dead onto the ground in plain view of the farm windows. I should perhaps point out at this juncture that pheasants were something of a grey area in terms of what we were authorised to shoot on the farm. The pigeons were wreaking havoc on the sprouts, since, with the whole of East Anglia buried under a carpet of snow, those sprouts were one of the few food sources still available to them, and the farmer was supplying us with free cartridges in return for our services in keeping the birds away from his crop. We certainly hadn't been told *not* to shoot at pheasants, but that hardly amounted to proper permission. Anyway: 'my' pheasant was now lying dead quite a lot nearer the farmhouse than was comfortable. We sidled gently in that direction, ready to execute a smart about turn at the sight or sound of the farmer. About a hundred yards from the farm we stopped and stood talking while one of the bolder spirits crawled along the ditch below the line of sight and popped out to snaffle the pheasant and conceal it under his jacket. Mission accomplished we sauntered off – looking the picture of innocence or so we hoped – to try to come to terms with some more pigeons.

In truth a pheasant was not exactly a rare bird in the village where I grew up. My parents ran a pub called the Four Horseshoes in Thornham Magna, a village on the Suffolk/Norfolk border. Lord Henniker, who owned the pub, and indeed practically the whole of the village as well, still ran his own shoot on pretty much traditional lines and

Walking up in a rushy field on a frosty winter morning.

the woods and fields were home to a very healthy population of wild pheasants and partridges. These though were very definitely off limits and I knew better than to risk parental wrath, not to mention the likelihood of an appearance in front of the Eye magistrates' court, by shooting at pheasants on the estate. The sprout field though was on a privately owned farm bordering the estate so my first cock pheasant, though he had almost certainly originated on Lord Henniker's ground, was at least borderline legal.

In fact, the next time we were speaking to the farmer he effectively gave us full permission to shoot game on the farm. We had gone to the back door of the farmhouse to scrounge a few more boxes of cartridges. I can still remember what he said as he handed over the cartridges. 'Don't you boys be afraid to have a go at a pheasant if you see one. Or anything else that gets up.' Funnily enough, to the best of my recollection, despite being given proper authority, I never shot another pheasant at Wood Hall.

I have shot quite a few pheasants since then – many more than I would have dreamed when I was a boy because pheasant shooting in those days was still pretty much the preserve of the relatively well off. In more recent times it has become far more accessible and with the growth of syndicate and commercial shooting it is within the grasp of anyone who would like to shoot pheasants and is prepared to spend a few pounds, to enjoy the sport at some level. Indeed, if you are prepared to go beating or picking-up in your spare time you may well be invited to take part in the end of season keeper's day and get a day or two out shooting at no direct cost at all.

Today, at the start of the twenty-first century, the pheasant is the mainstay of low ground shooting in the United Kingdom. A couple of hundred years ago things were quite different and the partridge reigned supreme over the lowlands with the grouse occupying top status on the hill. While the grouse, though much declined in numbers, is still the leading sporting bird of the moors and mountains, the partridge has declined to the extent that it is now numbered among the species described as 'endangered' by some conservation experts. Where Colonel Hawker regarded a bag of forty partridges over pointers to his own gun as nothing more than a fair day's sport but would muster all hands at the slightest rumour of a pheasant setting foot on his preserves, we now accept pheasants by the hundred and the thousand as perfectly normal, yet get excited at the sight of a single covey of partridges. And, attitudes having changed radically since the 1800s, we generally don't set out to annihilate the covey at the first opportunity as the good Colonel did whenever a pheasant was spotted.

The pheasant is such a versatile bird. Uprooted from its native jungle and introduced to Europe (and later, America and many other parts of the world) it thrives whatever the habitat. Flat, wet fenland, open farmland, rushy moors, dark, brooding conifer forests, airy deciduous woods, country gardens and town parks are all home to the pheasant and it seems capable of thriving and surviving in all of them. It will eat almost anything it can get into its beak, roost on the ground or high up among the branches, nest anywhere a hen can scrape out a place to lay her eggs and, if caught up and penned, settle down to a life in captivity with complete aplomb. Hatched in an incubator, reared under a heat lamp, fed chick pellets from day old and turned out into the woods seven weeks later with never a sight of a mother or a father, still it will adapt remarkably quickly to life in the wild and provide us with sporting shooting from October through to the end of January.

It is estimated that there are something like a million wild pheasants living in Britain and they are supplemented annually by somewhere around twenty million reared birds. Pheasant shooting is big business and the pheasant makes an enormous contribution to the economy of the countryside. The number of people employed, directly and indirectly in support of the pheasant must run into many thousands. There are the gamekeepers and shoot managers who organise and run shoot days, there are the beaters and pickers-up who are, in effect, the front line troops, plus the game farmers and feed merchants who supply the shoots with chicks, poults and the means to feed them, all relying directly on the sport for their living, but there are also many other trades benefiting indirectly from the pheasant.

Think of all the things we need – or think we need – in order to enjoy a day pheasant shooting. A gun and some cartridges, a cartridge belt or cartridge bag, a game bag or a game carrier, gun slip, snap caps, leg of mutton travelling case, cleaning rod, cartridge extractor, walking stick, shooting stick, hat, gloves, coat and breeks, boots, socks and quite possibly some thermal underwear, shirt, tie, scarf, ear defenders, safety glasses, hip flask, position finder, picnic basket, vacuum flask, trained retriever or spaniel, dog lead, dog whistles, spike to tie the dog down so he doesn't run in, electric collar to punish him if he does, a whole library full of books on shooting, shoot management, dog training, game keeping and pheasant rearing; four-wheel drive vehicle to carry all this clobber about in, dog cage so the hound doesn't eat the upholstery, kennel and run for the dog to live in when he is at home, clay pigeon trap for pre-season practice, gun licence, game licence and steel cabinet to store the gun in between times. Oh yes: and it helps if there are some pheasants.

The above is just a list of some of the things you can buy to enhance your enjoyment of your shooting. It doesn't include any of the equipment the gamekeeper needs in order to ensure that there are some pheasants for the beaters to send over your gun. The process starts with incubators and hatchers for the eggs. Then there are the chick boxes, rearing sheds, wood shavings for the floors, heaters, feeders, drinkers, plastic anti-peck bits, anti-biotics, wormers and tonics for the growing birds and poultry crates for transporting them to the release pen. Posts and wire for rearing pens and release pens, electric fences to keep away the foxes, feeders, drinkers, grids for the pop-holes, straw for rides, stock fencing around game crops and of course, the game crops themselves, sewelling for the flushing points, a quad bike for hauling feed around the shoot, straw for feed rides, rifle, lamp and squeaker for fox control, snares, Fenn traps, Larsen traps and mink cages to keep the birds safe from other predators, game cart and game larder, keeper's cottage and beaters' trailer complete with a Land Rover to tow it and, in this electronic age, probably a computer to keep your shoot records up to date and a website so your shooting clients can book their sport. As yet we haven't even touched on the hotels and guest houses, airlines, travel agents, sporting

Guns lined out ready for the start of a drive.

agents, ferry companies and restaurants needed to get our guns to and from the shoots and ensure their comfort while they are there. Let's just accept that there is more to pheasant shooting than a man, a gun and a pheasant.

So shooting is business – sometimes very big business – as well as sport. At one end of the spectrum may be the man who has the occasional walk round the hedgerows with the gun and the dog and considers he has had an excellent day if there is one pheasant in the gamebag at the end of it. At the other end is the commercial shoot manager with a budget measured in hundreds of thousands of pounds, organising forty or fifty or more driven days in a season, perhaps releasing sixty thousand birds and confidently expecting – indeed, relying upon – a bag of two or three hundred and possibly even more birds on every one of those shoot days. In between the two extremes are all manner of farm shoots and syndicate shoots run with varying degrees of efficiency, enthusiasm and professionalism. In most cases the shoot is organised so as to make the best use of the ground as it exists, though some of the more dedicated shoots spend a great deal of time and money altering the landscape so as to make it more suitable for the pheasants. New woods and hedgerows are planted, cover crops grown, conservation headlands and beetle banks established, farm crop rotations planned to maximise their sporting potential and tasks such as autumn ploughing delayed in order to boost the potential of the shoot.

Many of the best 'natural' woodlands so beloved of the conservationist lobby exist only because they were planted a century or more ago specifically to provide cover for pheasants and foxes for the benefit of those who shoot and hunt. It is a reasonable bet that any low ground landscape adorned with flourishing hedgerows and well-managed woodland will be host to a sporting shoot in one form or another and that the pheasant will be an important part of that shoot. This is not due to opportunism on the part of the shooters, moving on to land that just happens to be suitable for pheasant shooting. It is because, over many years, the land has been managed so as to enhance its suitability for sporting use. The fact that the end result happens to be a richly diverse environment that delights the eye of sportsman and anti alike and provides the ideal habitat for a whole variety of birds, animals and plants, many of which have no connection with the shoot, is simply one of the benefits that devolves from the influence of fieldsports on the countryside.

In today's politically correct society, where hunting, shooting, coursing and – in the near future if not at this precise moment – fishing are viewed with distaste by an ignorant minority of the population, and where the voice of that ignorance and prejudice is heard all too loudly in the Palace of Westminster, it is unfortunate that the truth about the importance of field sports to the countryside is either unknown to or ignored by many politicians. It is a sad reflection on the integrity of our elected leaders that they are prepared to overturn a whole way of life, not to mention the livelihood of several thousand people, in order to score cheap political points or to 'reward' their back-benchers for supporting, or at least not overturning, some other policy to which they are ideologically opposed. I never had a great deal of respect for the average politician, but the antics of the Blair administration over the past six or seven years has seen what little respect I might have had sink away to nothing.

But for the moment, and dare I hope, for the foreseeable future, we can still enjoy

Driven pheasants are the mainstay of winter shooting in Britain.

a day out shooting without incurring a criminal record. We can still fish, follow hounds, course a hare or ferret a rabbit – provided we have permission. My first pheasant may have erred on the side of illegality, but these days, being a respectable citizen, I take care to ensure that everything is above board before even thinking about firing a shot. A combination of personal preference and economic necessity ensures that pheasant shooting for me is invariably a low-key, low numbers affair but I am no less fond of the sport for all that. It would be a tragedy for the countryside as well as for those of us who are directly involved in shooting if it were ever to be banned because of the ignorance and blind prejudice of a few politicians.

But let us look at the sport in a mood of optimism. Shooting has never been more open and egalitarian than it is at the threshold of the twenty-first century. In particular, pheasant shooting is available for anyone who has the desire to take part and is prepared to make a small – or if they so wish, a large – investment to secure some sport. The pheasant may not be a true native of these shores, but it has been here long enough to be classed alongside the grey partridge and the grouse as a true representative of the very best of British sport. May we continue to enjoy it for many years to come.

2

THE PHEASANT

The pheasant, or *Phasianus colchicus* to give it the official title, is undoubtedly the most common and best known of all the sporting birds in Great Britain, and probably throughout the rest of the world as well. It may not be easy for the non-sporting person to distinguish between a partridge and a grouse for example, or correctly identify a mallard or a wigeon or a teal beyond the general classification of 'duck', but there can be few people who cannot instantly recognise and put a name to the pheasant.

In part this may be due to the exhibitionist tendencies of the male of the species. Grouse and partridge, snipe and woodcock are generally shy, retiring birds, but the pheasant, and in particular the cock pheasant, loves to strut about in full view of the whole world, and to advertise his presence with a loud and distinctive voice. And though the hen pheasant has relatively low-key plumage the brilliant – some might say gaudy – reds and golds of the cock positively scream 'Look at me' as he strides across a field. If the pheasant were a rare visitor to these shores the sighting of such a beautiful bird would surely draw bird watchers from every corner complete with their tripods and telescopes, high-powered binoculars and telescopic lenses. But because the pheasant is such a common sight in our countryside, and because the great majority of pheasants can be considered as semi-domesticated rather than truly wild birds, they are of little interest to bird watchers. No twitcher is ever going to feel a frisson of delight as he enters *Phasianus colchicus* in his lifetime species list. To the birdwatcher the pheasant is no more interesting than a domestic chicken.

And there is a certain rationale to that feeling since the pheasant and the chicken share a common ancestor in the red junglefowl *Gallus gallus*. There are around fifty different pheasant species living in the wild in their natural range which runs from the north-west of India through southern China and down the Malayan peninsular to the Pacific islands. The introduction of the pheasant to Britain is generally attributed to the Romans and for a bird that belongs in the jungles of the far east and reached us through the efforts of a people from the sunny Mediterranean it has adapted remarkably well to our far from tropical climate.

There is no question that the pheasant is instantly recognisable, but this is mainly due to its size and conformation since there are many variations of plumage. The hens are most easily described as brown, ticked with black, though the overall colour can range from a light sandy hue through to a burnt umber shading as dark as a grouse.

The magnificent plumage of a cock pheasant.

Additionally, the 'black' tips to the feathers are actually not simply black but deep, intense shades of blues and purples. In the cocks this variability is taken to even greater lengths.

The most commonly seen cock pheasant is the familiar reddish-gold bird with a dark green head and, perhaps, a white ring around the neck. But look more closely at one of these beautiful birds and you will find a whole host of colours hiding among the plumage. There is a brilliant ring of scarlet in the wattles surrounding the eyes. Then the head and neck are – what? So complex are the iridescent hues of the feathers on the head that they appear as different colours according to the angle at which they reflect the light. Let us assume our pheasant has a head of vivid metallic green. Then the sudden flash of pure white from the neck ring marks the change to the reds and golds of the neck and body. There are copper tones on the neck which lighten and

Cock pheasant resplendent in iridescent purples and blues.

brighten to become pure gold on the flanks. The breast feathers are almost black, the legs a duller brown and then the tail feathers are gloriously cross hatched with black bars over a ground that varies between copper and green. And that is just one variation on the general theme of cock pheasant.

Some cock birds lack the white collar around their necks: some have blue, or purple or almost black heads instead of green. The variety known as the Michigan Blue has a yellow/green crest on his head and soft, powder blue feathers on his wings and back. There are melanistic cocks that look almost solid black from a distance, though a close inspection will show them actually to be the deepest shade of bottle green or midnight blue. Occasionally a pure white bird will survive to adulthood. There are almost as many variations among the hens, though the differences are much more subtle in the sex that relies completely on camouflage to keep it safe while incubating eggs.

Great shot: a high pheasant cleanly killed.

This wide variety of plumage springs from the three or four different species of true pheasants that have intermingled to produce the mongrel variety that is the present-day bird with which we are all familiar. In some quarters the different types of bird are still known by the names of their forebears. The most common, red/gold bird is referred to as an Old English pheasant if it lacks the white neck ring, or as a Chinese Ringneck if it comes complete with collar. The predominantly greeny/blue cocks are sometimes called Japanese pheasants with the darker individuals known as melanistics. There is a certain amount of truth in these names, since our present hybrid mix of pheasants are primarily descended from four main true species. These are the Southern Caucasus pheasant *(Phasianus colchicus colchicus)*, the Chinese Ring-necked pheasant *(Phasianus colchicus torquatus)*, the Southern Green pheasant *(Phasianus versicolor versicolor)* which hails from Japan and the Mongolian pheasant *(Phasianus colchicus mongolicus)*. In practice, our pheasants consist of a jumbled genetic mixture and are really best described as mongrels.

There are three other varieties of pheasant that may be seen occasionally in the British countryside as well as the hybrid mix that is the common pheasant. They are all ornamental breeds: the Golden pheasant *(Chrysolophus pictus)*, the Reeves's pheasant *(Syrmaticus reeves)* and the Lady Amherst's pheasant *(Chrysolophus amherstiae)*. These may have escaped to the wild from collections or been introduced to parkland and estates to add a touch of exotic colour. The male Golden pheasant is an absolute riot of bright yellows, reds and golds with a golden cape, the male Lady Amherst's pheasant has blue/green wings and back, a silver cape, a flame coloured train of feathers on the rump, a black and white tail and white under parts, and the male Reeves's pheasant is characterised by a spectacularly long tail and golden/bronze plumage edged with black. The females of all three species are, as with the more common varieties of pheasant, much less flamboyantly coloured. In shooting terms none of the three are likely to figure in the bag, unless by mistake: and such a mistake will often be marked by a great deal of good-natured abuse from your fellow guns and, quite possibly, a hefty fine.

But let us leave such exotic creatures aside and return to the familiar sporting pheasant. The cock is a little larger than the hen measuring up to three feet from his beak to the tip of his tail, though that tail accounts for at least half the total length. The hen is considerably shorter at around two feet, though most of that difference comes from the longer tail of the male. The weight of an adult pheasant can vary from under two pounds to over four pounds. A brief weighing session of a few brace currently hanging in my larder had the cock birds averaging about three pounds four ounces and the females about a pound less, though I should emphasise that this was a very small sample. Additionally, the 'survey' took place towards the end of a remarkably good season when the weather was ideal at release time and on through the autumn so the birds were in exceptionally good condition with plenty of body fat. Wild pheasants are generally smaller than those released onto a shoot, probably because they have to work hard for their food rather than having it served up daily on feed rides or via hoppers.

Reared birds will typically be fed on proprietary pheasant food from day old until they are around twelve weeks of age, then gradually switched over to a diet of wheat.

They seem to thrive on this simple regime though most birds will supplement it with whatever edible matter they find available in the wild. The pheasant is far from a selective feeder and will eat practically anything it can get into its beak. Seeds of all kinds and fruits, from berries to fallen apples, grasses and leaves, nuts, insects, worms, slugs, snails, caterpillars, beetles and even things like mice and lizards will feature in their diet. Acorns and beech mast are particular favourites and can cause the gamekeeper problems during those years when they are plentiful because the supply of 'free' food means that the birds are not reliant on his hoppers or feed rides and are thus more liable to wander.

The pheasant is usually described as a bird of the woodland margins. The ideal pheasant country would probably consist of plenty of small woods with a mixture of deciduous trees and sufficient light penetrating the canopy to allow vegetation for cover and shelter to flourish on the woodland floor. The woods would border on arable fields with well established hedgerows, there would be ample supplies of water, stubbles would be left through the winter before being cultivated, and there would be a variety of crops grown including roots and kale as well as corn. Where such a situation prevails pheasants will flourish, but they can also exist quite comfortably in a variety of other much less promising habitats.

The pheasants of the fenlands of Norfolk, Lincolnshire and Cambridgeshire are well known for sporting excellence despite the flat open fields and dykes of the fens being far removed from the 'ideal' habitat of woods, hedgerows and fields. Shelter and concealment from predators are the two main requirements of pheasant habitat and where the birds lack access to woodland with good ground cover they will settle for

The pheasant is a bird of the woodland margins…

hedgerows, ditches, long grass, reeds and rushes, root crops, areas of set-aside, 'waste' ground and the like. If, in addition to concealment and shelter, a supply of food is readily available, pheasants can be induced to stay in some quite unlikely areas.

That said, the pheasant can be quite a notional bird when it comes to selecting a place to live. Sometimes the most unlikely seeming woods will attract and hold a good stock of birds while, on the same shoot, a wood that looks ideal for pheasants (from a human perspective) will be shunned by all except the occasional bird. The fact that pheasants are released in considerable numbers every year tends to distort the perspective of what type of habitat will 'hold' birds, and what type of habitat is unsuitable. Many shoots, by dint of good keeping and attention to detail, will release and hold large numbers of birds on ground where no truly wild pheasant would deign to show its beak. The fact that pheasants *can* be induced to live their lives in a particular area does not mean that the local countryside is ideal, or even marginal, pheasant habitat.

As we have seen it is estimated that there are approximately one million 'wild' pheasants living in Britain, but their numbers are supplemented annually with around twenty million released birds. It is a moot point as to how long a released bird has to survive, and how far it must roam from the point of release, before it is considered to be a 'wild' pheasant. In fact, since the pheasant is an introduced species (albeit the original introduction was two thousand years or so ago), it can be argued that there is no such thing as a 'wild' pheasant in Britain: only released birds which have gone native.

If the pheasant were not already established in Britain it would now be a criminal

...but can also be held on more open ground such as this shoot in Southern Scotland.

offence to introduce it. Under the Wildlife and Countryside Act, 1981, Section 14 (1) – Introduction of New Species, it is an offence for any person to release or allow to escape into the wild an animal which is:

1 Not ordinarily resident in or a regular visitor to Great Britain, or:
2 A Schedule 9 Part 1 species.

Schedule 9 Part 1 lists about fifty species of birds, animals, fish, reptiles and plants which are established in the wild in Britain but which may not be released. The logic behind this ruling is presumably that some releases/escapes of exotic species have caused severe problems for native species – the grey squirrel, the Sika deer and the Zander spring to mind. It was this legislation that made it illegal to put down Chukar, or Red-legged/Chukar hybrid partridges after 1988, prior to which they could be released under general licence. Incidentally, among the species to which Section 14 applies are the Golden, Reeves's, Lady Amhersts's and Silver pheasants, so it is no use thinking you can add a touch of colour to your game cart by putting down any of these exotic varieties. Had such legislation existed during Roman and Norman times then the pheasant would not exist in Britain at all.

It can be argued that this might not be a bad thing. Until the middle of the twentieth century the grey partridge flourished in the British countryside. Changes in farming practice, particularly the increasing use of pesticides and herbicides coupled with the destruction of thousands of miles of hedgerows, caused a steady and inexorable decline in the numbers of partridges living wild in our countryside. Along with the partridge many other species of farmland bird found themselves struggling: skylarks, lapwings, curlews, sparrows, buntings, finches... the list is enormous.

As the number of partridges declined it might have been expected that the shooting fraternity would have made strenuous efforts to find the reason and reverse the situation, and indeed, I am quite sure that is exactly what would have happened if it had not been so easy to replace the partridge as our major low ground game bird with the ubiquitous pheasant. Because pheasants are relatively easy to rear, release and to hold within the boundaries of a shoot, because they are quite predictable in their habits and can, with not too much difficulty, be persuaded to fly over a line of guns, and because shoot owners could pretty much arrange their shooting to order, with reared pheasants in whatever numbers they chose, rather than relying on the partridges' natural cycle of abundance and scarcity to control their sport, it was all too easy for the decline in partridge stocks to be ignored. Bags slowly changed from being comprised mainly of wild partridges to a mixture of partridges and reared pheasants, and then to the current situation where the majority of shoots rely almost entirely on reared pheasants for their sport.

It is in no way my intention to denigrate the pheasant as a sporting bird. A high pheasant curling across the wind can be as sporting – for which read 'difficult to kill' – as any game bird. The fact that pheasants can thrive in such a variety of habitat means that shoots can be organised on ground where it would be difficult, if not completely impossible, to hold a stock of partridges. For the small shooting syndicate working on a tight budget and leasing whatever ground is available, the willingness of the pheasant to adapt and compromise is a blessing. Even if the land is farmed in a manner that is far from game friendly, shooting can still be organised. In contrast, the partridge is a much harder customer to satisfy and quite likely to vote with his feet if he doesn't care for the habitat where you wish him to establish himself.

And there lies both the advantage of and the problem with pheasants. Because good sport can still be organised despite the environment being degraded to the extent that wild game such as the grey partridge can no longer thrive, it is only natural that the reared pheasant should replace the wild partridge as the main low ground quarry. Unfortunately the problem doesn't stop there. Prior to the advent of modern agribusiness farming methods produced an environment that naturally suited the grey partridge. Incidentally, those same 'old-fashioned' ways of farming and the wide diversity of habitat that resulted from them are slowly coming back into fashion as cheap imports and short-sighted Government policy make farming an endangered way of life. Those stocks of partridges were maintained and increased by means of good game keeping: preservation of habitat, control of predators, minimising of disturbance during the nesting season and ensuring that there were sufficient supplies of natural food available to allow the birds to rear their chicks. Good game keepering though is a very labour intensive occupation, and the very time when the traditional keeper was

In the early days of muzzle-loaders partridge and grouse were the main quarry for the sporting gunner.

Pheasant poults dust bathing on the rearing field.

at his busiest is the same time when the pheasant keeper is fully occupied catching up, incubating, rearing and releasing his pheasant poults.

As the numbers of partridges fall, accompanied by a corresponding rise in pheasant numbers, so the keeper is more and more occupied with his rearing programme and less and less able to spend time encouraging the wild bird population. And, as the numbers of wild birds fall, so it becomes less cost-effective for the keeper to spend time on them. Twenty hours a week trapping, plus several thousand pounds spent on developing beetle banks and conservation headlands might put a hundred wild partridges into the bag during the course of the season. The same expenditure of time and money could well mean an extra thousand pheasants shot. The arithmetic is simple and where shoot budgets are tight the outcome inevitable.

Ironically, the partridge is now making something of a comeback at the expense of the red grouse. Grouse numbers have been declining steadily for many years. In direct contrast to the case of the partridge this decline has taken place despite the most strenuous efforts to identify the cause and rectify the matter, and despite the system of moorland management staying broadly the same as it was during the golden years of grouse shooting. In much the same way that the pheasant replaced the partridge on farmland some shoots are compensating for the lack of grouse by releasing partridges onto moorland.

The system is simple enough. Partridge poults are trickle released from a number of small pens, spread across the moor. Their natural inclination to bond as a covey means the first birds released will stay close to their release pen so as to maintain contact with the birds still inside. By the time all the birds have been let out they should have become hefted to the area around their pen, thus creating an artificial covey system with groups of birds spread all across the moor.

They happily seek cover in banks of bracken, so that invasive weed becomes an asset instead of the liability that it is to grouse keepers. I must confess that I have mixed feelings about using moorland for releasing partridge, even though it is something that I do myself on a small shoot in which I have an interest. There is no denying that releasing partridges onto the lower margins of a moor is a means of guaranteeing shooting for the owners, providing work for keepers and even taking some of the pressure off the grouse population. However: there is also the danger that, because releasing partridges is, disasters excepted, a means of providing a guaranteed number of shoot days for the owners, the whole effort of the shoot will be directed to partridge management, thus hastening the decline of the grouse, in exactly the way in which the rise of the pheasant contributed to the demise of the wild partridge.

The pheasant is a ground nesting bird, the hen scratching a hollow in the ground and lining it with a sparse covering of vegetation to make a rudimentary nest. The nest site is usually in some sort of cover: brambles, rushes, long grass, the base of a hedgerow, under a pile of brushwood or fallen tree or among a patch of nettles. Wild hens are said to be far better in their selection of a nest site than the survivors from birds released the previous autumn and also to make better mothers, though I have not seen any scientific research that either confirms or contradicts these assertions.

In the spring pheasants move out from the woods into more open country as they begin their mating rituals and this is no doubt why so many shooting men complain that, having seen very few birds during the season, the ground is apparently overrun with them as soon as 2 February dawns and they know they are safe from law-abiding sportsmen if not from all their other predators. In their native lands the cocks are usually monogamous but in Britain a rather peculiar system has evolved with both cocks and hens establishing territories independently.

A cock will establish and defend an area of several acres, depending to some extent on the density of birds left at the end of the shooting season. The hens meanwhile form small groups and move around an area that may encompass the territories of several cocks, and will mate promiscuously with several of these males. Eventually a hen will settle down to lay around a dozen green to olive brown eggs, though as many as twenty have been recorded from a single bird. Sometimes more than one hen will lay in the same nest, and on occasion a hen pheasant will lay her eggs in a partridge nest. Foxes and crows are particularly hard on sitting hens and their eggs during this most vulnerable period and they are also easy pickings for mink and roaming dogs. The hen normally incubates the eggs and rears the chicks with no help from the cock, though this is not invariably the case. A pair of pheasants nested a few yards from our home when we lived in Sutherland and used to come with their brood to feed among our chickens, and the cock was always present, keeping a lookout for predators and shepherding the chicks into cover when any sort of danger seemed to threaten.

Hen pheasants are reputed to be poor mothers. It is claimed that, where partridges are aware of the whole of their broods, a hen pheasant is quite happy as long as a single chick accompanies her, often wandering off and leaving several of her chicks behind, lost and alone. From my own observations I can verify that partridges will indeed go to tremendous lengths to keep all their chicks safely close by, and it is certainly true that any hen pheasants that I spot with good numbers of chicks will usually have considerably less of a brood the next time our paths cross. Whether this is because of a general failing in the hen pheasants' mothering instincts I cannot say. It does occur to me though that a partridge is considerably smaller than a pheasant and also more used to living in the open under the eyes of various predators. A hen pheasant is a big bird and one that is much more easily seen than a partridge, and it may just be that crows, foxes, cats, stoats and weasels, birds of prey in general and anything else that cares to make a meal of a pheasant chick find it relatively easy to spot a pheasant with her brood and home in for a free lunch.

One factor that may influence the degree to which reared pheasants are successful in raising a brood is the amount of food available to them in late winter and early spring. Released birds are often almost completely reliant on the food provided for them on feed rides or in hoppers during the shooting season. If this supply is abruptly

A cock pheasant for this gun while walking up with his spaniel in late autumn.

cut off when shooting ends, just at the time of year when natural food is most scarce, it is likely that these birds will find it harder to find an alternative source of nourishment than wild birds that are used to fending for themselves. If you do have a reasonable stock of birds left at the close of the season, and if time and shoot funds will permit, then the cost of a few extra bags of wheat may be more than repaid with a bonus of 'free' birds next season.

Not only will a regular supply of food help to maintain the fat reserves of the hens for when they are sitting on their eggs and thus unable to spend much, if any, time foraging, but it will also encourage the birds to stay on your ground and may even entice straying birds from around about to take up residence. The cost/benefit calculation is a simple one. The cost of putting a pheasant in the bag is somewhere in the range of £10 to £15. Spend £100 on a ton of wheat and if it helps bring just a dozen extra birds to your bag the next season you have more than justified your outlay.

The old method of rearing pheasants before the advent of game farms was for the keepers to collect up eggs and set them under broody hens. This was extremely labour intensive. If we assume that one broody could raise twenty pheasant chicks it would obviously take fifty to produce a thousand poults. On those estates where a single day's bag would be expected to exceed a thousand birds the keepers would have been in charge of literally hundreds of coops, each with its broody hen that would have to be let out, fed and watered every day until the chicks were hatched – when the even harder work would begin.

Instead of simply ordering a ton of chick crumbs from the feed merchant part of the keepers' remit back then was to prepare his own mash, boiling up meal, meat and spices every day and quite possibly having to shoot or snare rabbits by the hundred to supply the protein content of the meal. It was normal for a keeper to live on the rearing field for three months every year, bedding down in a rough shed or an old caravan and working, literally, from daylight to dark.

Nowadays we can order our poults ready to go to the wood direct from the game farm at seven weeks old. Their food comes ready bagged to go straight into the hoppers and the miller can supply it treated with various forms of medication against parasites and disease. An electric fence will help to keep the birds safe from foxes, dogs and cats and most keepers will have a Land Rover or a quad bike to take the hard work out of humping wheat around the feed rides. Even so, looking after a pheasant shoot, however satisfying, can still mean long hours and hard work, usually for fairly meagre wages in comparison with many other jobs. The rewards though, in terms of job satisfaction, can be considerable, and on a crisp winter day when the pheasants have flown high and fast, the beaters have worked happily and efficiently and the guns have shot well there are few keepers who would change their profession no matter what the financial inducement.

The pheasant may be an interloper: a foreign import brought to these islands by an invading army a couple of thousand years ago, but, I sincerely hope, the pheasant is here to stay. Whether he is curling high above the guns at a driven shoot, strutting about in springtime in the full glory of his breeding plumage, or nestling on a plate surrounded by roast potatoes, green peas and glazed carrots, he is a bird to delight the eye, the taste buds and the sporting instincts.

3 GUNS AND AMMUNITION

A gun, brought right down to basics, is no more than a metal tube, sealed at one end and open at the other. If a measure of gunpowder with some form of projectile on top is placed in the closed end and ignited, the rapidly expanding gases given off as the powder burns will force the projectile out of the open end of the tube at a rate of knots. And, if you are at a pheasant shoot and the tube happens to be pointing in the right direction, the result should be a dead pheasant.

The earliest guns were indeed little more than metal tubes, loaded by having powder and shot poured into their muzzles, rammed down to the closed end, and then fired by igniting the powder with a slow match applied to a hole in the barrel wall. Crude though they were, they were dangerous weapons both to the intended victim and to the gunner since they had an unfortunate tendency to explode and scatter shards of hot metal in all directions. Despite this lack of reliability the gun soon became established as a weapon of war, and as the value of the gun as a battlefield weapon became evident further development was swift to take place. Man has always been keen on finding new and more efficient ways in which to kill his fellow man. Improvements centered around three main areas – speed of loading, accuracy and ease of ignition. As far as the shotgun is concerned, firing a large number of projectiles spreading out over a considerable area, and with its strictly limited range, accuracy of the degree required of rifles and cannon is not particularly important. Speed of loading and ease of ignition definitely are though and it was in these areas that improvements were made.

Early weapons were generally, though not exclusively, muzzle-loaders. Some cannons employed a crude form of breech loading, but the overwhelming majority of weapons from the great cannons employed on warships and battlefields, through military muskets and rifles, right down to tiny pocket pistols, were loaded through their muzzles.

The process was inevitably slow, though it is said that a British infantryman at the time of the Napoleonic Wars could fire three or even four shots per minute – spurred on no doubt by the sight and sounds of a French column with swords, muskets and fixed bayonets advancing on him with murder in their minds. Various means were employed to try and speed up the loading process. Musket ammunition was pre-packed in a paper cartridge containing powder and bullet. To load, the infantryman bit off the end containing the bullet and poured the powder down the barrel, reserving a pinch to 'prime the pan' (the pan being the part of the lock which held the powder that was ignited by the flint striking the steel hammer). The paper case was screwed up and pushed into the muzzle to act as an over-powder wad; then the bullet was dropped in behind it and forced home with the ramrod. All that remained was for him to lift the rifle from the ground and haul the cock back, bring it to his shoulder, aim and fire. If the target was several thousand troops marching in a column, shrouded by smoke, at a range of twenty yards or so, then taking careful aim was pretty much optional. The target was too big to miss and possibly invisible anyway.

Powder for cannons was sewn into cloth bags containing a measured charge. Once a bag had been rammed down the barrel a sharp point was thrust through the touch-hole to pierce it thus enabling the powder to be ignited by a touch from a slow match, a spark from a flintlock or from a reed filled with gunpowder placed in the touch hole. Every little refinement helped to speed up the re-loading process, but even though a few seconds might be shaved off each cycle the fact remained that charging a musket, pistol, rifle or cannon was a slow business. Regular practise would reduce the time taken, and the fact that the Royal Navy and British infantry regiments practised regularly with live ammunition is often cited as a major factor in the victories at Trafalgar and in the Peninsular War. Even so, loading a weapon through the sharp end was never going to be a swift process. Inevitably, the muzzle-loader gave way to the breech loader.

The principle was, and is, simple. You package the various components of your cartridge in a tube – paper, cardboard or brass were the usual materials employed (though plastic has now largely replaced all three) – and then, instead of ripping it apart and pouring the contents in sequence down the muzzle, you open the other end

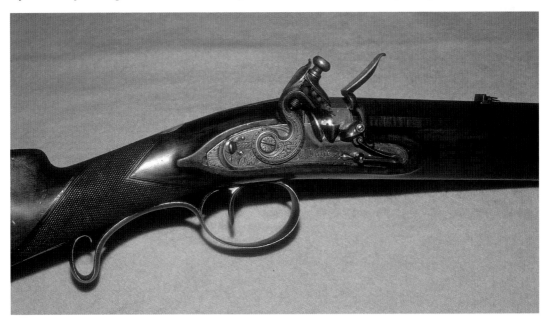

Early days: a fine flintlock rifle.

Re-loading a muzzle-loader was a slow process.

of your gun and pop the whole cartridge into the breech. Close the gun again – some sort of hinge works well with smaller, hand-held weapons, or a screwed breech-plug in the larger ones – and then all that remains is to ignite the charge. It was an invention that improved the means of ignition that finally allowed the change from muzzle loading to breech loading to come about.

The percussion cap was developed by the Reverend Alexander Forsyth in about 1805. Instead of the flint and steel arrangement of the flintlock, a tiny copper cap which held fulminate of mercury was placed over a hollow nipple and made to explode when it was struck by the hammer, thus sending a flame down the touch hole to ignite the powder. The early percussion guns were still muzzle-loaders and took just as long to charge as a flintlock. However, once the hammer fell, ignition was both faster and more certain. Flintlocks were notoriously unreliable, particularly in the wet, and even when they did fire there would be a measurable delay between the flint striking sparks from the steel, the sparks igniting the powder in the priming pan and finally the ignition of the main charge. With a percussion cap instead of a perceptible delay between pulling the trigger and firing the shot, action and reaction became virtually instantaneous.

A cloud of smoke as this percussion muzzle-loader is fired.

The next, logical step was to combine the percussion cap, powder, wads and shot or bullet into a single casing. This quickly led, via pinfire and rimfire configurations, to the modern, centre-fire cartridge. Once the principle of breech-loading was established there was swift progress in the development of the shotgun, principally in the design of the locks, the means of automatically clearing the breech of spent cartridges and ways of improving the ease with which the gun could be opened and closed in order to speed up further the process of re-loading. By the third quarter of the nineteenth century gun making had progressed from the muzzle-loading flintlocks in use at the time of Waterloo to the modern, double-barrelled, hammerless ejectors that we use today. Indeed, there are still many guns in regular use that were built before the start of the twentieth century and are every bit as effective – perhaps even more effective – than many modern weapons.

A gunsmith might beg to differ over matters of detail, but the sporting shotgun has changed very little in the past one hundred and thirty odd years. For the purposes of shooting pheasants, at least in Britain, we can pretty much ignore all the single-barrelled variations of the shotgun, whether they are single shot, pump action, bolt action or semi-automatic, and concentrate on the two types of double-barrelled weapon available: the side by side and the over and under.

These terms apply to the orientation of the barrels: whether they are arranged on a horizontal (side by side) or vertical (over and under) plane. Both have been around for a long time, although until relatively recent years virtually all game guns were side by sides, with over and under guns reserved almost exclusively for clay pigeon shooting. Indeed: there were some shoots where an over and under was barely acceptable and might attract some funny looks from your fellow guns if you turned up

The pin-fire was the forerunner of the modern, centre-fire cartridge.

intending to use one. Today this unwarranted stigma has vanished and either configuration is equally acceptable almost everywhere.

As to which you should choose if you are buying your first sporting shotgun I can offer only limited guidance. It is said that the single sighting plane of the over and under makes it inherently more accurate than the twin barrels of the side by side. This may or may not be true, and even if it is generally correct, may not be true in your particular case. You may find that you, personally, will feel happier and shoot better with a side by side than an over and under. Over and under guns tend to be a little heavier than side by sides and may be very marginally slower to reload since the barrels have to drop down further than those of a side by side in order to allow the fired cartridge from the lower barrel to clear the face of the action when it is removed. Whether this will ever make a difference to your success and enjoyment of pheasant shooting is a moot point.

If you are buying a new gun and don't have any fixed preference between the two configurations I would suggest that you handle as many as possible of both and, if it can be arranged, try out the ones that appeal to you on some clay pigeons. Many clay shooting grounds will arrange for you to borrow a range of guns and can combine your testing with a shooting lesson and advice on gun fitting. If you form a particular preference then that is the type of gun to buy: if not, then be guided by the depth of your pocket, the guns that are available, and whatever takes your fancy in the gunsmith's shop. Remember: if you don't get on as well as you had hoped with your choice it is a simple matter to trade it in and try something different. Shotguns, particularly good quality shotguns, tend to appreciate in value over time, provided they are looked after properly.

Old-fashioned but still effective in the right hands. A grouse killed on a muzzle-loading day.

Besides the orientation of the barrels there are a number of other decisions that must be made regarding your preferred choice of a new gun. They are all essentially compromises because it is impossible to design the perfect gun for all occasions. That which is ideal in one situation may be found lacking in another. In order to appreciate the reasons why you must choose between one option and a number of others we should first consider a little simple physics; specifically Newton's Third Law of Motion which states that 'For every action there is an equal and opposite reaction'.

Let us consider the limitations of the shotgun as a weapon. The reason we are using a shotgun, which fires a large number of very small projectiles called shot, instead of a rifle, which fires a single, larger projectile called a bullet, is because we are trying to hit a moving target. To kill a bird in flight with a single bullet would require marksmanship of the very highest order, plus a considerable measure of luck. It would also be a very dangerous thing to do because of the distance at which a bullet is dangerous compared to shot. A typical shotgun load of an ounce or so of shot will travel perhaps a quarter of a mile at the most, and by the time it has covered that quarter of a mile it will be no more dangerous than being pattered on by a heavy shower of rain. A one ounce bullet could well be capable of killing a man at a distance of a mile or more if anyone was so foolish as to start firing a rifle indiscriminately up into the air without knowing where the bullet might come back to earth.

When the shot charge first leaves the muzzle of a shotgun it consists of a tightly packed bunch of pellets that starts to spread out, and string out, as soon as it is free of the constriction of the barrel. These dual actions of spreading and stringing are what

Take the 'big load of heavy shot' theory to its logical conclusion and you end up with a punt gun.

give us a sporting chance of hitting a moving target. The shot forms a column that steadily widens and lengthens the further it travels from the muzzle of the gun. The width and length of this shot column allows us a margin of error in our aim that would not be available if we were firing a single bullet. However: because each individual piece of shot is very small the range at which a shotgun retains the power to make a clean kill is severely limited.

Major Sir Gerald Burrard did a lot of work between the first and second world wars to try and establish the effective range of the shotgun and in 1931 published the results of his experiments in a book called *The Modern Shotgun*. By calculation and experiment he worked out the combination of number of pellets and the striking energy of each pellet that would be required to make a clean kill on various types of quarry. For example, he surmised that small birds like snipe needed to be struck by at least two pellets, each having a striking energy of at least 0.5 ft lb, whereas a large bird such as a goose would require four pellets, each having a striking energy of at least 1.5 ft lb to ensure a clean kill. These are his calculations of the *minimum* requirements: in practice more – perhaps many more – pellets may strike the quarry. It must also be considered that 'freak' kills can occur when a single pellet strikes a vital spot even though *in theory* the quarry is out of range.

Note that there are two components to take into consideration: the number of pellets striking your quarry, and the force with which those pellets strike home. Both factors vary according to the distance from gun to quarry. The shot charge exits the muzzle as virtually a solid ball of shot travelling at something over one thousand feet per second. At point blank range that closely clumped ball of shot has sufficient energy to kill an elephant, never mind a snipe or a goose. At fifty yards both snipe and goose may be beyond the effective range of the gun. The elephant certainly will be. It all depends on the individual size and total weight of shot used in the charge, plus the degree to which it has spread out - and this is where we have to start making compromises.

Our expectation when shooting with a shotgun is not that we will kill our quarry with a single, well-placed projectile striking a vital organ as is the aim of the rifle-man, but that several individual pellets will strike the target and in combination deliver sufficient shock and tissue damage to ensure a quick, clean kill.

Whole books have been written about the effective range of shotguns. In general, any discussion of the range of shotguns centres on their *maximum* range. At twenty yards virtually any shotgun and any combination of shot load will kill any normal shotgun quarry, be it snipe, goose, hare, rabbit, duck, grouse or pheasant – provided only that the gun is pointed in the right direction. At fifty yards, a distance that is commonly quoted as the 'maximum range' of a sporting shotgun, all or none of them might be in range, depending on the amount of shot you were using and the size of the individual pellets.

While it is not strictly correct in practice, we will assume for the sake of our deliberations that a given weight of shot will spread out to cover a similar area at any given range irrespective of the size of the individual pellets. Shot sizes are denoted by numbers or letters. Number 9 shot is quite small: number 1 much larger, and certain very big shot sizes are designated by letters such as BB or AAA. An ounce of number

1 shot will contain approximately 140 pellets: an ounce of number 5 about 220 and an ounce of 8s around 450. These, incidentally are British denominations: American and continental cartridge manufacturers use the same numbers for slightly different sizes of shot. For the purposes of pheasant shooting most guns will use 5s, 6s or 7s for reasons that will become clear shortly.

Imagine a charge of shot leaving the muzzle of a gun and progressively spreading out and stringing out as it travels towards your quarry. The more it spreads the greater the margin of error in aiming that will still allow you to hit your target. If the pattern is twenty inches across you are clearly more likely to miss your target than if it is forty inches across. Obviously then, we will want the shot to spread out as widely as possible, won't we? Probably not.

The wider the spread of the shot the more space there must be between the individual pellets. Remember that we are hoping to hit our quarry with several pellets; not just a single one. Therefore, if the shot charge has spread out *too* widely it may no longer have sufficient density to hit our quarry with enough pellets to ensure that clean kill which we are striving to achieve. We may even miss the quarry altogether, even though we have pointed the gun in the right direction because there are big enough gaps in the pattern for it to fly through unscathed. Therefore we must either reduce the spread of the shot string or use more pellets *either* by loading a heavier charge of the same size shot or by employing the same total weight of a smaller size of pellets.

Except that things are not quite so simple. Remember that killing our quarry cleanly depends on both the number of pellets that strike it *and* the striking energy of each individual pellet. Striking energy is a factor of the weight of the individual pellet and the speed at which it is travelling. Obviously, while the weight remains constant, the speed of the pellets decreases as they get farther from the gun. The larger the pellet the more striking energy it will have as it leaves the muzzle, and the more striking energy it will retain at any given range.

So: to summarise all that. Small shot sizes help to ensure that we have a dense enough pattern to be sure of hitting our target with several pellets if we are accurate in our aim but they may lack the individual striking energy to ensure a clean kill. Large shot sizes retain sufficient striking energy to ensure a clean kill at a greater distance, but by then may have become so thinly spread that we are no longer certain that an accurate shot will hit our target with enough pellets to bring about the desired result. Presumably then, what we must do is load our shotgun with a heavy load of big pellets and thus enjoy the advantages of both a dense pattern and a high striking energy?

Let us return to some basic physics and Newton's Third Law of Motion which states that for every action there is an equal and opposite reaction. In the case of the shotgun this means that the momentum of the recoiling gun is equal to the momentum of the issuing change. Now, momentum equals weight x velocity, therefore the weight x the velocity of the shot as it leaves the muzzle will equal the weight x the velocity of the recoiling gun. Put simply, the heavier your load of shot the more energy it will require to propel it out of the barrel, and thus the harder your gun is going to kick.

The most basic method of reducing the effect of the recoil is by making the gun heavier. Therefore it would appear that the simple answer to producing a gun that will be effective at the greatest possible range against whatever quarry we chose to pursue is to build a big, heavy gun that will fire a big, heavy charge of shot. And if your only criterion were to produce a gun that would kill at the maximum possible range then a big heavy gun would probably meet your requirements. Wildfowlers, who seek their sport on the foreshore and expect to take just the occasional shot at big birds like geese at long range, do indeed arm themselves with just such weapons: ten bores and eight bores, twelve bores firing three inch magnum cartridges and the like. Taken to its logical conclusion this theory produces the punt gun: a miniature cannon firing up to a pound and a half of shot. While such a weapon will certainly maximise the range of a shotgun it is hardly suitable for pheasant shooting.

Even if the effects of recoil are discounted, it is generally true that a gun designed to throw a heavy shot charge will itself be heavier than one designed to throw a light load, if only because the extra force required to propel the heavier charge means that the barrels and action of the gun must be made strong enough to cope with the higher pressures generated. As a very rough guide it has been calculated that a shotgun should weigh ninety-six times the weight of the shot load it is intended to fire in order to reduce recoil to an acceptable level. Thus a gun designed to fire a one ounce load should weigh six pounds: a gun intended to fire an ounce and a quarter load would weigh nearer to seven and a half pounds.

In practice there is much more to the perceived effects of recoil than just the weight of the gun and the shot load. A badly fitting gun that catches your cheekbone may recoil with no more force than a gun that fits you perfectly, but it will certainly feel as if it is kicking a lot harder. When shooting under field conditions, with all your attention on the quarry, you may not be conscious of any recoil at all. Firing the same gun and cartridge combination at a pattern plate, with no distraction in the form of a flying pheasant, may leave you uncomfortably aware of the gun's kick. In addition, some propellants, despite achieving the same result in terms of muzzle velocity of the shot charge, may be quite different in the perceived recoil they produce. Perhaps surprisingly, it appears that faster burning powders appear to kick less than more progressive propellants.

But let us leave theory and extreme forms of shooting aside and return to our choice of a gun for pheasant shooting. What are our requirements?

On a rough shoot, ten miles walked and half a dozen shots fired might represent a decent day's sport. At a driven shoot where the bag is around two hundred birds, each of eight guns might well fire in the region of a hundred or more shots. A very light gun that was easy to carry might be a good choice for the former, even if it did give your shoulder a good whack with every shot. The same gun, used on the driven day, might well leave you with a sore shoulder and an aching head. Our first compromise therefore is to select a gun that will be light enough to carry but heavy enough to reduce recoil to the level at which it will be pleasant to shoot for the number of shots that we expect to fire on any one day.

Then there is the question of range. Our earlier considerations were mainly looking at the *maximum* range of a shotgun. In practice, on the great majority of pheasant shoots, very few pheasants will be killed at extreme ranges. Most will be shot at a much shorter distance – between twenty-five and thirty-five yards is a reasonable estimate. If we design a gun with tightly choked barrels, firing a heavy load of large sized shot we will certainly maximise our range, but by restricting the spread of the shot we will also make it harder to hit the birds that fly past at normal distances. Even worse, those birds we do succeed in killing at median ranges may well be hit by so many pellets that they will be unfit for the table.

There is more. It is only on the very best of driven shoots that you are likely to be challenged by a pheasant gliding fifty yards above your peg, and it is only the very best of shots who are likely to be capable of killing it. If you equip yourself specifically to have the capability of killing the bird that you only see once or twice in a season you will, at the same time, be handicapping yourself when it comes to hitting those that fly over you the other ninety-nine per cent of the time. The very fact that you are rarely challenged by a really high bird in itself reduces your chances of hitting one when it does cross above your peg. Your gun might be capable of killing the bird but the odds are you will miss anyway. If though, you shoot regularly over ground where very high pheasants really are the norm, then there is an obvious case for buying a gun that is capable of dealing with them.

Bore

The first consideration is likely to be the bore of the gun. The bore of a shotgun (with the exception of the smallest gun normally used in the field, the .410 (or 'four-ten' which has a bore .410 inches in diameter) is described by a number, viz twelve bore, sixteen bore, twenty bore and so on. The number relates to how many perfectly spherical balls of lead with a circumference that fits exactly into the barrels would make up one pound in weight. Thus a one ounce ball of lead, being a sixteenth of a pound, would have the same diameter as the barrel of a sixteen bore shotgun, and obviously, the lower the number the bigger the bore of the gun.

The twelve bore is undoubtedly the most common gun in use on pheasant shoots and indeed practically every other type of shoot. Even wildfowlers on the foreshore, where heavy loads are the norm, are most likely to use a magnum twelve. It is also the biggest gun that you are ever likely to find at a pheasant shoot, though it is just possible that you may come across the occasional, slightly eccentric shot using a ten bore. The next most common size is the twenty bore, followed by the sixteen bore: these smaller bores having been enjoying something of an upsurge in popularity over the past few years.

Although it is possible to find very light twelve bores or heavy twenty bores, in general the smaller the bore the lighter the gun will be, and the lighter the load of shot it will throw. A 'typical' (if I may employ an inexact term) twelve bore game gun will weigh around seven to seven and three-quarter pounds, and be designed to fire between an ounce and a sixteenth and an ounce and three-eighths of shot. You can buy twelve bore cartridges loaded with less than an ounce of shot or with an ounce and a half or even more, but for normal pheasant shooting the standard twelve bore load is between an ounce and an ounce and a quarter, with the former being considered a light load and the latter a heavy one.

A twenty bore load will normally be between three-quarters of an ounce and an

The standard English game gun: a twelve bore, sidelock in use at a spaniel field trial.

ounce, with a sixteen bore ranging between seven-eighths of an ounce and an ounce and a quarter. Using the rule of 'ninety-six times shot load' we can estimate that a twenty bore can be built to weigh as little as five and a half pounds: a twelve bore will probably be over seven pounds and a sixteen bore somewhere in between the two. Note that this is in no way a rigid rule: there are heavy twenty bores and light twelve bores widely available, just as there are heavily and lightly loaded cartridges made to fire through both.

It is important to understand that the larger bores are not more *powerful* weapons than the smaller bores. The velocity of the shot leaving the muzzle of a twelve bore will be no greater than that from a four-ten, and the striking energy of an individual pellet will be exactly the same. The greater range offered by larger bores is attained because they fire a bigger shot load that provides a denser pattern. Therefore one ounce of shot, which is a *light* twelve bore load, will offer exactly the same performance (for all practical purposes) when it is fired from a twenty bore, where it would be considered a moderately *heavy* load.

There are slight differences in the way a shot load performs dependent on the shape of the original shot column: i.e. the cylinder formed by an ounce of shot in a twelve bore cartridge will be wider and shorter than the same ounce of shoot loaded into a twenty bore cartridge and this will make a slight difference to the way in which it spreads and strings out in flight. The longer shot column in the twenty bore also means that more pellets are in contact with the barrel walls and are thus liable to be damaged by abrasion. Finally, the smaller the bore the smaller the area at the base of the shot column on which powder charge can exert its force. Therefore, to accelerate a given charge to the same velocity as in a larger bore the smaller bore must operate at a higher, or more sustained pressure. This too will have a detrimental effect on the quality of the pattern.

It is possible to buy twenty bore cartridges loaded with a shot load of an ounce and a quarter or even more, but you will have to pay for this extra performance in the form of considerable, and possibly unacceptable, recoil. My personal view is that there is little point in trying to squeeze twelve bore performance out of a twenty bore. If you want a light, fast handling gun then a twenty bore may be ideal for you and, using standard twenty bore loads of just under an ounce of shot, should deal perfectly adequately with ninety-nine percent of pheasants – provided you point it in the right direction. If you prefer a slightly heavier gun then a standard twelve bore will offer you rather more flexibility in your choice of loads and will, in theory at least, be marginally more efficient in its performance.

That said, a good shot with a small-bore shotgun will always kill far more pheasants than a poor shot with a larger one.

Choke

Shotgun barrels are not made in the form of a simple cylinder of uniform diameter. Because the pressure generated by the burning powder is far greater at the breech than at the muzzle, gun makers can reduce the weight of a gun and improve its balance by making the barrel walls progressively thinner from breech to muzzle. This is what gives a shotgun barrel its typical tapering appearance, even if the internal diameter is constant throughout the length of the barrel. In practice, very few modern shotguns are constructed with barrels of constant internal diameter or 'true cylinder' boring, most having some degree of choke.

Choke is the term used to describe the way in which shotgun barrels are restricted at the muzzle. The result of this restriction is to reduce the amount by which the shot spreads once it has left the barrel. There are various degrees of choke, denoted, in order of increasing restriction as Improved Cylinder, Quarter Choke, Half Choke, Three-quarter Choke or Full Choke. In a twelve bore shotgun full choke equates with approximately forty thousandths of an inch restriction at the muzzle: half choke with twenty thou, and improved cylinder with around five thou. Alternatively, choke can be defined in terms of the percentage of the shot load that will be contained within a thirty inch circle at a distance of forty yards, and in a fully choked gun this would be around seventy percent as compared with a true cylinder barrel where the amount of shot in the circle would be closer to forty per cent, or a half choke barrel with sixty per cent.

By tightening up the pattern, choke boring increases the effective range of a shot load. We have seen earlier that, even though each individual pellet still retains sufficient striking energy to be effective against a particular quarry, after a certain range the pattern may have become so spread out that there is no longer any certainty that a correctly aimed shot will kill the quarry. By applying a degree of choke to a barrel the distance at which a pattern remains effective can be increased.

As an illustration, at fifty yards true cylinder boring should put just under thirty per cent of a shot load into a thirty inch circle. A full choke barrel would put almost fifty percent of the same shot load into that circle. By using choked barrels therefore, we can either use a heavier shot size, which retains a greater striking energy, and still hit our quarry with enough pellets to ensure a clean kill, or, by dint of the tighter pattern, strike our quarry with more of the same size of pellets, than if we were using a true cylinder gun. Choke boring does, unquestionably, extend the range of a shotgun with any given shot load, and the tighter the choke the further the range will be extended.

By how much can we extend the range of our gun? Let us assume that we have calculated that, in order to ensure a clean kill on a pheasant, using number six shot, we need a pattern that has one hundred and twenty pellets spread evenly across a thirty inch circle. An ounce and an eighth of number sixes will contain approximately three hundred pellets, so, according to this particular calculation, the effective maximum range of our gun for pheasants is the distance at which it will group forty per cent of its charge into that thirty inch circle. If the gun is bored true cylinder that distance is forty yards: with half choke it is fifty yards and with full choke it is fifty five yards. So: provided that individual pellets have retained sufficient striking energy at fifty five yards to kill a pheasant, having our gun bored full choke will give it an effective range some fifteen yards longer than that of a true cylinder gun.

But inevitably there must be some sort of trade off for the increased range. Choke boring increases the density of the shot pattern by restricting its spread. At thirty yards – and on many shoots you will shoot a lot of pheasants at this sort of range – the true cylinder barrel will have a shot spread of just under four feet: the full choke barrel just

Really high pheasants may require heavy loads and tight chokes…

…but most pheasants are shot at much shorter ranges.

over two feet. In effect, at this range true cylinder doubles your margin of error when measured against a full choke barrel.

And we should also consider the condition of the game you are shooting. At thirty yards a full choke barrel will put practically every one of those three hundred pellets of number six shot into a thirty inch circle. If you hit a pheasant squarely in the centre of your pattern it will be so riddled with shot as to be virtually inedible. Tight choking therefore, though it will certainly increase the distance at which you *can* kill a pheasant, is unlikely to increase the *number* of pheasants you kill – unless the great majority of your shots are taken at birds near the extreme range of the gun.

Let us take another look at an almost identical scenario, but substitute number seven shot for the sixes we used in the first example. With around three hundred and eighty pellets in an ounce and one eighth load the distance at which the required one hundred and twenty pellets will strike our thirty inch circle is extended to forty-five yards for true cylinder barrels and sixty yards if they are bored full choke. However: the smaller pellets have a lower striking energy than the sixes used in the first example. Number six shot will have a striking energy of just over 0.8 foot-pounds at fifty-five yards, which is the minimum that Burrard recommends for pheasants. Number sevens though will fall below the minimum necessary at distances beyond forty-five yards. In other words, an ounce and an eighth of number seven shot will *in theory* be no more effective in a full choke barrel than it will in one bored true cylinder since it retains a sufficiently dense pattern to kill a pheasant right to the point where the striking energy of the pellets falls below the minimum required in either case.

There are virtually limitless combinations of choke, shot load and shot size, and there are high velocity cartridges available that will increase the striking energy of the pellets and thus extend your range a little further. In theory – and I must emphasis the words 'in theory' – if you fire an ounce and a half load of number five shot through a full choke barrel you should be able to kill pheasants cleanly at sixty yards. Whether you can hit a pheasant at sixty yards is another matter, and what that same load would do to a pheasant at twenty-five yards is best forgotten. In theory, a true cylinder barrel firing an ounce of number seven shot should maximise your chances of killing every pheasant that flew over your peg, up to a distance of forty-five yards. At the same time, it would mean that those real screamers: the ones that really make your day when you happen to kill one cleanly in front of the whole line: would all be out of range.

In theory you can devise shotgun loads to suit all sorts of circumstances. If the type of ground you shoot over is such that your pheasants are generally low birds then a twenty bore shotgun with improved cylinder barrels firing three-quarters of an ounce of number six shot might be the ideal gun for you. Another shoot, where the birds are consistently at the very limits of shotgun range might require an ounce and a quarter of number five shot fired through fully choked barrels to maximise your chances of killing birds cleanly. The problem is that, in practice, in the course of a single days pheasant shooting you are quite likely to be presented with birds at both twenty-five and fifty-five yards range, and a whole lot of others in between.

Just to make things more difficult, you have no way of knowing whether the next bird over your peg will be a fifty-five yard screamer or a much lower, but still perfectly shootable, bird at perhaps thirty yards high. The cartridges in your pocket, belt or bag are probably all from the same box, with exactly the same shot load, so even if you knew in advance whether the next bird would be high, medium or low you wouldn't have the facility to switch to the most appropriate weight and size of shot anyway.

It is quite possible to specify a particular combination of bore, choke and shot load to meet a particular circumstance. I have a friend who runs a big commercial shoot in the Borders, showing magnificently high pheasants: pheasants so high that some of his clients claim that they are out of range. In order to prove that his birds are killable he sometimes joins the line with his twenty-eight bore gun and proceeds to kill the highest of pheasants with apparent ease. The secret, of course, is that he is an exceptionally fine shot, and the twenty-eight bore is choked as tightly as his gun maker could contrive. The point is made though that the problem for the guns is not that the pheasants are out of range, but that they are just too difficult to hit.

Actions

Shotguns are made in various configurations. The simplest are single barrelled, single shot weapons, and then there are several different types of single barrelled repeating guns: pump actions and bolt actions that are reloaded physically, plus recoil and gas operated semi-automatics that eject the fired case, replace it with a loaded cartridge and cock the action so that subsequent shots can be fired simply by pulling the trigger. All have their merits, but for all practical purposes guns used for pheasant shooting in Britain are double barrelled either in side by side or over and under configuration.

In fact, if you shoot alone or perhaps with one friend, walking up your pheasants with just your dogs for company, then a single barrelled shotgun, whether of the single shot or repeating variety may be an acceptable choice of weapon. At the great majority of pheasant shoots though you will be expected and perhaps even required to shoot with a double barrelled gun. This is not just a matter of snobbery or fashion but is dictated by sporting ethics, custom and, most importantly, safety.

If we exclude the occasional oddity like the French Darne action where the barrels slide forward rather than dropping down when the gun is opened, one feature of all breech loading double barrelled guns is that they can be held and carried with the barrels broken (i.e. in the open position), demonstrating quite clearly to anyone in the vicinity that there are no cartridges in the chambers. Thus, if eight or ten shooting men are standing around chatting between drives with their guns over their arms, provided that all the guns are broken, it is patently obvious that they are safe. Pumps and semi-automatics cannot easily be shown to be empty and for this reason alone they are not welcomed on the majority of shoots. The sight of one or more closed and, as far as you are aware, loaded guns pointing at your kneecaps is not calculated to add to your peace of mind and enjoyment of the day.

On the practical side, a conventional break action shotgun provides its owner with a much quicker and easier method of reloading between shots than any of the rapid firing single barrel guns where cartridges have to be fed into some form of magazine. In Britain, where the magazines of all repeating shotguns are limited by law to holding only two cartridges (unless they are registered on a firearms certificate), a double barrelled gun will allow the operator to keep up a greater sustained rate of fire than a pump or semi-automatic simply because it is much, much faster to reload. Indeed, even if it were still legal, and acceptable to your fellow guns, to load five cartridges into the magazine, although those five shots could be fired rapidly, an experienced shot with a double barrelled gun would still be capable of a greater sustained rate of fire once the first five shots had been expended.

There are two main kinds of hammerless shotgun action: the boxlock and the sidelock, though within the two categories there are many individual variations in design. The boxlock mechanism is built into slots machined out of the action body and is a simple, sturdy and well-tested design. Sidelock shotguns have individual firing mechanisms let into the stock and action on either side of the gun and are generally a more complicated and more elegant design than the boxlock. In addition there are trigger plate actions, where the firing mechanism is attached to the trigger plate, primarily found in the Dickson roundaction shotgun. There are even hammer guns available for those who may wish to revert to the weapons of a previous era. All, apart from the hammer guns, work on the same general principle.

A hammer gun was readied for firing by the gunner pulling the hammers back and thus utilising his own strength to store energy by compressing the springs that would then be used to fire the cartridges. When a hammerless gun is opened and closed, the weight of the barrels and the leverage of their movement is used to compress the springs that operate the firing mechanism and the ejectors and, in the case of game guns, to reset the safety catch to the 'safe' position. By using the action of opening and closing the gun to cock the internal hammers the process of reloading is speeded up relative to that of a hammer gun, since as soon as the hammerless gun is closed it is ready to fire.

Few shots now use hammer guns for pheasant shooting. They are perceived by many as being inherently dangerous because of the possibility that the hammer could slip when being cocked or lowered, particularly with cold, wet hands. To some people a gun with the hammers drawn back into the full cock position looks dangerous. It is worth remembering that hammerless guns are *always* at full cock (unless they have just been fired) since the very act of opening and closing the gun cocks the internal hammers. Applying the safety catch *does not* mean that the gun is safe: only that the triggers are locked. Dropping the gun or giving it a sharp blow can be sufficient to jog the hammers and let them fall, causing an accidental discharge. A hammer gun with the hammers lowered will not go off by mistake. Hammer guns may look threatening but, handled properly, they are no more dangerous than any other weapon. They are though very rarely seen on formal shoots these days and it might be difficult for anyone using a hammer gun, particularly if he were a novice, to gain acceptance from his fellow guns.

Whole books have been written about the relative merits of boxlock and sidelock actions. In general so-called, 'best' guns are built on the sidelock principle. The sidelock is a slightly more complicated mechanism and has a more elegant appearance than the often chunky look of the boxlock. In addition most sidelocks include an intercepting sear which prevents the gun being fired accidentally if the hammer is released by a jolt such as might occur if the gun were dropped or given a sharp blow. The sidelock is said to offer superior trigger pulls and to be easier of access for cleaning purposes. However: these claims need to be approached with a degree of caution since a good boxlock will be a far better gun than a shoddily made sidelock.

Sidelocks and boxlocks alike are available in a wide range of prices and quality. You could easily pay £50,000 for a best sidelock by a top English maker, but you could also pick up a low-grade, second-hand sidelock for as little as £100. They would clearly not be of comparable quality. Equally, there are top-grade boxlocks on the market which carry price tags in excess of £20,000 and others that would leave you change from £100. From the point of view of the pheasant that gets caught in the centre of the pattern it will make no difference at all whether the gun that fired the cartridge cost a small fortune or was picked up for a fiver as an unwanted lot at an auction. It will still be a dead pheasant. The cheapest gun will potentially have the same range, the same rate of fire, the same accuracy and the same amount of recoil as the most expensive. Is there any point therefore in spending more than the absolute minimum necessary to purchase a shotgun for pheasant shooting?

Is there any point in buying a Rolls-Royce or a Ferrari when a second-hand Ford will serve exactly the same purpose? Why buy an expensive cashmere topcoat when a plastic mac will keep the rain off just as efficiently? What makes a collector pay a fortune for an original Picasso when a good copy could be obtained for a tiny fraction of the price and would be indistinguishable from the original to anyone but an expert? The answers, if indeed there are any answers, are complex and vary according to the individual concerned.

It may be the aesthetic pleasure of owning an example of outstanding craftsmanship. It may be a desire to own the very best that money can buy; the wish to impress your friends, or the fact that certain items, including good quality guns, often appreciate in value far more rapidly than many more conventional investments. It may simply be the desire to own a particular gun regardless of whether it is necessarily the best or the most rational choice. If we were being coldly logical and measuring the value of a gun only by its efficiency in killing pheasants then it would be very difficult to justify buying anything more costly than the cheapest gun that was a reasonable fit.

If a gun throws a decent pattern, more or less fits you and is neither too light nor too heavy for your style of shooting, then you will kill as many pheasants with it as your ability allows, no matter whether you paid £50 or £50,000 for it. The answer to the question of whether there is any justification for buying an expensive shotgun is, therefore, that there is none whatsoever – *provided that you are making that judgement solely on the efficiency of the gun in killing pheasants*. As soon as you begin to factor in personal preferences, the extra satisfaction of owning an object that is beautiful in form as well as function, the desire to invest money in an asset that will appreciate, the wish for maximum reliability and the simple, human wish to possess one particular object rather than another that is superficially similar, then a whole range of non-objective choices enter the equation.

The best sidelocks are unquestionably more expensive than the best boxlocks. Aesthetically and mechanically they can probably be fairly labelled better guns. Under field conditions it is unlikely that even the most discerning shot would notice a difference between their performance. The choice of action therefore is best left to the individual preference of the purchaser, to what is available within his price range and to what 'feels right' when he is making his decision. Confidence is vital to good shooting, and being happy with your choice of gun, whatever the reasons, can only serve to enhance it.

Ejectors

Nearly all sidelocks and a fair percentage of boxlocks are equipped with selective ejectors: devices that throw out the fired cartridge cases as the gun is opened but leave loaded cartridges in the chambers. In non-ejectors part of the rim of the chamber levers the cartridges outwards when the gun is opened in order to allow them to be grasped easily for removal by hand. Obviously, the ejector system gives a significant advantage over the non-ejector where speed of re-loading is concerned. If you are shooting on the kind of driven shoot where large numbers of birds cross your peg in rapid succession ejectors are almost essential. Even if you only fire half a dozen cartridges in a day there is a certain satisfaction in hearing the spring of the ejector and half-glimpsing the spent cartridges flicking over your shoulder – and there will always come the day when you *need* to re-load quickly because you are in a hot spot and getting two more cartridges into the chambers with maximum speed is suddenly the most important thing on your mind.

It should also be said that more and more shoots are, quite rightly, asking guns to pick up their fired cartridges. With a non-ejector the spent cases are already in your hand as you reload and can slipped into a pocket or dropped in a tidy heap at your feet to recover at the end of the drive. Unless you hold your hand behind the chambers and catch your cartridges when using an ejector you may well find it difficult to recover them after the drive, particularly if you are standing in long undergrowth or crops such as turnips, kale or beet. You can rest assured that they will be glaringly obvious to the farmer the next time he walks across the field. Finally, though a well made modern gun is a model of reliability, the ejector system is one more thing that *can* go wrong.

Triggers

Double guns are built with either one or two triggers. The conventional arrangement is to have two triggers with the front trigger firing the right hand barrel of a side by side or the upper barrel of an over and under. This allows you to make an instant choice of which barrel to fire – useful when your gun has different choke in either barrel, or if you have loaded different shot sizes, perhaps at an end of season fox drive where you have sixes in the one barrel in case a pigeon comes over and BBs in the other ready for a fox. You also have the advantage of having two independent sets of firing mechanisms. If one fails mid-drive you can still shoot on using the gun as a single barrelled weapon.

Some double-barrelled guns are equipped with only one trigger, though you are more likely to find this particular set-up in guns designed for clay pigeon shooting. There is usually a selector switch that can be slid across to determine which of the barrels fires first, i.e. top/bottom or right/left. These single trigger or single selective trigger guns are possibly marginally quicker in getting off the second shot than a gun with two triggers, but their design is complicated and thus prone to failure. It should be noted that most single trigger guns will not fire the second barrel if the first suffers a mis-fire.

Self-Opening Guns

A self-opening gun incorporates a spring system that causes the gun to open simply by operating the top lever. Those guns with a conventional action have to be opened using the right hand to operate the lever and the left hand to pull down the barrels. The advantage of a self-opener is that it affords the possibility of much faster reloading.

Normally, having fired a shot, a gun will be opened using the right thumb to operate the top lever while the left hand pulls down the barrels, then will be held by the left hand while the right reaches into the pocket or down to the belt for fresh cartridges, slips them into the chambers, then grasps the stock ready to close the gun. With a self-opener the left hand can be reaching for cartridges even as the gun is opening and the used cases are being ejected. This saving in time may not seem very great, but if there are pheasants streaming over your head in great numbers having a self-opener *and being practised in the appropriate reloading technique* could make a significant difference to the number of shots you are able to fire at any one stand.

There is a price to pay in return for this speed because all the springs: for the hammers, the ejectors and the self-opening mechanism: have to be compressed when the gun is closed and it will take noticeably more effort to close a self-opener than a conventional gun.

The 'Right' Gun

We have taken what is no more than a very brief glimpse at some of the factors that we may consider when selecting a gun for pheasant shooting. I use the word 'may' advisedly because there are two extremes of gun purchasing technique with a whole range of possibilities in between. At one extreme you get in touch with someone with a gun for sale – through an advertisement in the local newspaper perhaps – and you buy what is on offer. Alternatively, you could visit a gun maker, be measured using a try gun to establish the perfect fit for you, specify everything: bore, choke, weight, barrel length, action, number of triggers, type of stock and the chunk of walnut from which it will be made, pattern of engraving, fore-end, rib, chequering, butt plate and a

The over and under shotgun is now common and quite acceptable at nearly all pheasant shoots.

dozen other tiny details: then wait a year or two for it to be custom built. Most of us will never be able to afford the latter, but we will probably make a little more effort at finding the right gun than simply grabbing the first that is offered.

So what is the 'right' gun for pheasant shooting? The first and most important thing to establish is that the gun you buy is a reasonable fit.

A shotgun is not aimed at a target in the way that a rifle is employed. To hit a moving target the gun has to be fired some way ahead of the target in order to compensate for the distance the target travels in the time it takes for the shot to get from the gun to the point of impact. Instead of aligning the gun on the target quite deliberately by using some form of sight, when shooting at a flying pheasant (or a running rabbit or a clay pigeon or any moving target) in theory we should simply bring the gun up to our shoulder while concentrating on the quarry and pull the trigger. If the gun is a proper fit it should automatically be pointing at the spot where our eyes are looking.

In order to make a gun a proper fit for an individual shot there are several factors that a gunsmith can build in to a new gun or – to some extent – alter on an existing one. These are primarily concerned with the angles made between the stock and the line of the barrels, plus the overall length of the stock. The two main angles to consider are the degree to which the butt of the gun falls below the line of the barrels when viewed laterally, and the amount by which the barrels are cast off (i.e. angled away from a straight line with the stock) when viewed vertically. (Cast off means the barrels are aligned to the right of the line of the stock, for a right-handed shot. If the gun is to be fired from the left shoulder the barrels should be cast on, i.e. aligned to the left of the stock.) Thus a gun designed for a right-handed shot will have a stock that is angled down from and to the right of the line of the barrels.

If barrels and stock formed a perfectly straight line then pointing the gun instinctively would mean that, for a right-handed shot, it would be aligned above and to the left of the target. If you imagine mounting that straight line gun and holding the stock steady while angling the line of the barrels to point at the target you would end up with a shape like that described above – and that is pretty much the shape of most conventional shotguns. It is the degree of bend that determines whether a gun is a suitable fit for an individual.

The amount the stock drops below the vertical will determine how high or low the gun shoots. The degree of cast off will control the lateral movement of the point of impact. The length of the stock will compensate for the build of the shot: whether his arms are long or short: and the angle at which he inclines his body when taking up his shooting stance – in effect, how square on to the target he stands. It should be noted that different instructors may have different views on the correct stance and the proper way to mount a gun. What is important for the beginner is to find a stance that is comfortable for him, that correctly aligns the gun with the target, and that he can reproduce time after time after time: even when pheasants are pouring over in numbers and he is feeling more than a little bit flustered.

If a gun fits properly then it should come up sweetly into the shoulder and place the centre of its charge squarely on the target without the operator having to adjust his stance or the angle of his head in order to accommodate any less than perfect measurements of the gun itself. In practice, most of us learn to make little adjustments in our stance so that we can hit our target: in other words we fit ourselves to the gun rather than the other way round. This is far from the ideal, but we live in a practical world and for many shots this is a perfectly acceptable compromise.

The complete beginner is in something of the classic chicken and egg situation when it comes to selecting a gun. A correctly fitted gun will point at the target automatically *when it is properly mounted to the shoulder*. It follows therefore that the would-be shot must learn to mount a gun correctly before he can establish whether that gun is a proper fit for him. However: many novice guns start off by purchasing their first shotgun and then set out to learn the proper way of using it. The best way for a complete novice to get an introduction to shooting is probably to visit a clay pigeon shooting ground and have a lesson or two from a competent instructor.

That said, a much more usual way of selecting a gun that is the 'right fit' is to dry mount it a few times with both eyes looking at a target point, then close one eye and check that it is pointing at the target. An alternative is – having checked and double-checked that the gun is empty – to mount it with the eye of an accomplice as the aiming point and allow him to ascertain if the gun is actually pointing where you intend.

An awful lot of guns are bought with no more testing than two or three practice mounts in the shop or the back yard of the seller. Such a brief survey may well be all that it is practical to do, but it offers no guarantees. Although the gun, when dry

A wide choice of guns available from a trade stand at a game fair.

mounted, may appear to be aligned perfectly with the target it is possible that the barrels may not centre their charge exactly on the point at which they appear to be aimed. This can be checked by testing the gun on a pattern plate, mounting and firing a few shots at a mark without taking conscious aim and seeing whether the shot pattern is high, low or offset to one side.

Dry mounting the gun will give you a rough idea of whether it fits or not. Testing it on a pattern plate will help to confirm this initial assessment. Ideally though, you should try to arrange to test the gun on a clay pigeon range, under the eye of an experienced instructor, to discover whether it is really a good fit in practice as well as in theory. A competent gunsmith can make minor adjustments to the bend and drop of the stock: it is relatively simple to shorten the stock or to lengthen it, and even to build up the comb with a cheek pad. These though are considerations that may follow once a gun has been chosen. Let us now consider what might be the right gun to choose for pheasant shooting.

The first thing to understand is that there is no such thing as a universal 'right' gun for pheasant shooting. The gun that suits one man may not suit another. It is impossible to lay down hard and fast rules about what is right and what is not right, so all that I will be doing is trying to guide you towards a choice of gun that will be suitable for your purpose. We will assume that you are going to shoot driven pheasants since that is how the majority of pheasants are presented to the guns, and we will assume that you don't start out with any firmly fixed preferences as to bore or choke. If, like my friend from the Scottish Borders, you have a strong inclination for a tightly choked twenty-eight bore, plus the ability to use it effectively, then a tightly choked twenty-eight bore is the right gun for you, no matter what advice you may receive to the contrary. Those with more flexible views should read on.

The first thing to determine is the bore – and for all practical purposes this means either a twelve, sixteen or twenty bore. I would go further and suggest that, unless you have a reason, rational or otherwise, for preferring a sixteen bore, or perhaps have been offered the chance to buy a suitable gun in this gauge, your selection is likely to be either a twelve or a twenty bore. I am not suggesting that there is anything wrong with the sixteen bore, but since it is considerably less common than the twelve and the twenty you are less likely to be offered a suitable gun in this size. There is also the possibility that in some parts of the country you may experience problems in getting cartridges unless you order them specially.

The twelve bore is the standard workhorse of shooting sports. It is versatile, universally popular, eminently suitable for pheasants and virtually every other branch of sporting shooting. Twelve bore cartridges are available everywhere in enormous variety, and no matter where you go to shoot a twelve bore will be completely acceptable.

However: you may prefer a lighter gun, because of your age, because of some physical limitation, or simply because you prefer a light gun. In this case the obvious alternative is the twenty bore since it is likely to be a lighter gun than a sixteen bore. There may be some individuals who will decry the twenty bore and suggest that it is not really suitable for pheasant shooting, but, in the hands of a competent shot, it is just as capable as a twelve bore of killing ninety-five per cent of the pheasants you are likely to encounter. Remember: the velocity of individual pellets leaving the muzzle of a shotgun will be exactly the same irrespective of whether that gun is a four-ten or a four bore. Extra range is achieved because the bigger bores can fire more pellets of any given size, thus maintaining an effective pattern over a greater distance.

Lightness of itself is not necessarily desirable in a shotgun. If you are going to do a lot of walking in the course of your shooting then there is certainly a case to be made for a light gun. However, many shots perform better with a heavier gun, perhaps because the extra weight helps to maintain their swing and prevent them poking at birds. Less weight also exacts a price in the form of more recoil, and in some cases – ladies and young shots for example – a little more weight may be an acceptable trade off in order to reduce recoil. A standard twelve bore firing a light load (for a twelve bore) of one ounce of shot is likely to be a much sweeter shooting gun than a light twenty bore firing the same one ounce load.

Guns carried broken (open) are demonstrably safe.

A twelve bore is also a more versatile choice than a twenty. While it is true that a three inch chambered magnum twenty bore *can* handle shot loads of up to an ounce and a quarter, unless it is relatively heavy it is unlikely to be a pleasant gun to use with those maximum loads, particularly if you are firing a lot of shots in a short time. Most twelve bores will handle an ounce and a quarter load with ease and a three inch magnum will cope with anything from an ounce to an ounce and three-quarters of shot – though again, it is likely to be a heavy gun if it is designed to handle the biggest loads. Avoid the temptation to buy a twenty bore and then try to turn it into a twelve bore by pumping heavy loads through it. A twenty bore should be a light gun firing a relatively light load. If you want to fire loads of over an ounce a twelve bore will do it better and be a nicer gun to shoot into the bargain. Unless you have a particular reason for selecting a twenty bore I would suggest that a twelve bore is likely to be a better choice for a first gun.

The other major consideration is the amount of choke in each barrel. Briefly, choke increases maximum range by restricting the lateral spread of the shot charge. A true cylinder barrel will limit the distance at which you can kill a pheasant, but, unless you are an exceptionally good shot, it will also increase the number of pheasants you kill within the effective range of the gun. Full choke will maximise the range at which you *can* kill a pheasant but it will also make it slightly more difficult to *hit* that pheasant at all ranges.

One advantage of having two barrels is that you can have different amounts of choke in each thus offering an instant choice of choke. Conventionally, the right barrel, which is normally fired first, has less choke than the left. This may have been logical when game was walked up or shot over pointers because, with the birds flying away from the gun, the second shot would usually be taken at a longer distance than the first. Now consider a cock pheasant, rising in the wood in front of you and sailing directly above your peg. Your aim will be to kill that pheasant out in front, so your first shot will probably be taken when he is perhaps thirty yards ahead of you and thirty yards high – total range, according to Pythagorus, about forty-two yards. Let us assume that you miss with that first shot; the pheasant keeps coming; and you get a second barrel away just as he is vertically overhead. Total range now will be only thirty yards. Which shot called for the tighter choke under those circumstances?

Let us consider another instance. We will assume that you killed that cock pheasant cleanly with your first shot. He was not alone though and a second pheasant is following on roughly the same flight path just a few yards behind him. There is no time to reload so you swing onto the second pheasant and fire your second barrel at the optimum moment when he is thirty yards ahead and thirty yards high – exactly the same range as the first bird. Surely, if (say) improved cylinder is the 'right' amount of choke for the first pheasant, then improved cylinder is also the 'right' amount of choke for the second.

But what if that first pheasant had been a real screamer at forty yards high instead of just thirty? If you try to kill it when it is thirty yards in front of your peg the actual range would be fifty yards – possibly too far unless your barrels are fully choked. So you wait until he is nearly straight over your head and 'only' forty yards away before you fire that first shot. If you miss now and spin round to try a second shot behind the

A challenging bird but eminently shootable whatever the choke and calibre of the gun.

line the range will be increasing with every yard the pheasant glides and more choke will be the order of the day for the second barrel.

All of which is more likely to confuse than to help make a rational decision about how much choke is required in each barrel. The answer cannot be simple because what is ideal for one circumstance will be completely wrong for another. My feeling is that, for the average shot and the vast majority of pheasants, something like improved cylinder in both barrels would probably yield the best results overall in terms of kills to cartridges. A competent shot who anticipates the chance of a significant number of genuinely high pheasants might be better served by a bit more choke – perhaps improved cylinder in one barrel and half choke in the other, or quarter choke in one and three-quarters choke in the other. Only if you are going to be regularly tested by the very best of high pheasants should you consider full choke in either or both barrels. It may mean that, on paper, you are equipped to deal with the birds that cross your peg at the very limits of shotgun range, but the chances are that you won't be good enough to connect with them anyway, and you will also have made it harder to kill those birds that fly over at more realistic heights.

One other consideration. It is normally a simple job to reduce the amount of choke in a shotgun barrel, but it is very difficult to increase it. If you find a gun that suits you in other ways but is bored too tightly for your taste there should be no problem in getting some of the choke taken out.

So what about the question posed at the start of this section? What is the 'right' gun for pheasant shooting? Is there such a thing at all? The honest answer is probably not, in that the gun that would be the perfect choice for rough shooting with your spaniel might be less suitable at a formal, driven shoot. The tightly choked gun needed to deal with exceptionally high pheasants driven over a Devon valley could be far too much gun for a more modest shoot on the flat lands of Norfolk or Lincolnshire. If you spent the price of a small house on a best English gun you might hesitate at the idea of being a walking gun where 'walking' meant thrusting through thorns and brambles in order to shoot pheasants coming back over the beating line. If your budget is strictly limited the 'right' gun for you is unlikely to be a top-grade sidelock. So what would be a reasonable compromise? Let us try to make a summary of what we have been considering.

The first and perhaps only essential is that the gun is at least a reasonable fit. You are never going to shoot successfully with a gun that is pointing a foot low and a yard to one side when you bring it into your shoulder. After that practically everything is down to individual choice.

If you are going to shoot in company then your choice is almost certain to be a double-barrelled gun for both practical purposes and to satisfy convention. Whether you chose an over and under or a side by side is a matter of personal preference. The over and under is said to improve accuracy for some shots but a lingering prejudice against this configuration may still exist on the odd shoot.

I would suggest that you select the minimum amount of choke that will deal comfortably with the quality of pheasants that you will *normally* be shooting rather than trying to equip yourself for the once in a season screamer or the once in a lifetime invitation to test yourself against the very best of high birds. Of course if your regular diet consists of pheasants forty and fifty yards above your peg your definition of 'normal' will be different from mine and you should amend your choice accordingly.

Single selective triggers are more complicated and less common than conventional double triggers. Switching from one system to the other can be difficult and leave you either tugging futilely at the trigger guard as you reach for a non-existent second trigger in one case, or wondering why the front trigger is not firing the second barrel in the other.

Ejectors are not essential but they certainly allow you to reload faster and even on the most modest shoots there will be occasions when you want to get another pair of cartridges into the barrels in the shortest time possible. That said, in most cases the pheasants that wasn't shot because you couldn't reload in time may well be there next time you go shooting. And you might have missed it anyway. If your shoot insists on you picking up your fired cartridges – as it should do – then ejectors make this task a little more difficult.

Self opening and easy opening actions are desirable refinements if you can afford them and may shave a few milliseconds off your reloading sequence, but the lack of them will hardly spoil your shooting days.

There is virtually no practical advantage in selecting either a sidelock or a boxlock. A well built gun in either format will last you a lifetime if you clean it properly and treat it with care. A badly made gun is a badly made gun no matter what action it employs. The sidelock should be a little less prone to going off accidentally if you start dropping it or bouncing it around, but you're not going to do that, are you?

Straight hand stocks, pistol grips and semi-pistol grips are another area where individual choice is the only guide to selection. If it feels comfortable and you can shoot with it then it is the right style of stock for you.

So what would I buy if I were about to purchase a new gun for pheasant shooting? A side by side, because side by sides are what I have used all my life. If it were to be my only gun then a twelve bore would just get the nod over a twenty bore because it would give me a little more versatility, particularly in view of my choice of choke. This would be improved cylinder in the right barrel and then I would haver between having quarter choke in the left or having it bored improved cylinder as well. It would have two and three-quarter inch chambers so that I could partly compensate for the open boring by using an ounce and a quarter loads if anyone was kind enough to invite me to shoot really high birds, but for my normal shooting I would stick to standard cartridges.

I've used double triggers all my life, so the new gun would have double triggers, and it would be an ejector to help me out on those odd moments when there are several pheasants in the air all at the same time. Those are my basic requirements. From now on we are looking at things that are desirable rather than practical as far as my personal choice is concerned.

Most of them are to do with form rather than function. In practical terms it doesn't make a scrap of difference what the gun looks like as long as it shoots properly. Aesthetically though, a well made gun is almost a work of art, and the satisfaction that comes from shooting with it is out of all proportion to any actual benefits of performance. A well figured piece of walnut for the stock, sharp, well defined chequering, simple but beautifully executed engraving and crisp trigger pulls may not make me a better shot but they will add an indefinable something to the pleasure I get from shooting, and the only reason I shoot is because I expect to enjoy it.

My first choice, if price were not a major consideration, would be a Dickson round action twelve bore shotgun: a design that has always struck me as both elegant and practical and, when compared with a Purdey or a Boss, not overly expensive. (My bank manager might have a different opinion.) You may have entirely different aspirations: an over and under twenty bore, single trigger, fully choked Browning or Berretta perhaps. If so, then your choice is every bit as valid and practical as my own. I hope we both get what we want one day and find that it is as good as we hoped.

Cartridges

When I started shooting cartridges were made of rolled paper. Opening a new box of cartridges used to release a distinctive aroma that hinted at winter evenings flighting pigeons in the woods or crisp, frosty mornings bolting rabbits with a ferret. The fired cases also had their own particularly evocative smell of burnt powder that seems to be lacking from modern cartridges. The old cartridges had to be kept dry, otherwise the paper would swell and the cartridge would not fit into the chamber or, more often, would remain stubbornly stuck in the chamber after firing. Quite a lot of shooting men included a cartridge extractor in their shooting kit as a matter of course. The modern cartridge is made of plastic and doesn't swell up or suffer from damp. It doesn't decompose readily either and can cause injury and even death to farm animals if chewed and swallowed. Left to litter the fields or woods they will remain an affront to the eye for many years. Picking them up and disposing of them properly is not exactly difficult and every shooting man should ensure that he does just that.

The majority of modern cartridges also include a plastic cup that acts as a wad and as a means of protecting the shot from abrasion against the barrel walls. In the case of cartridges loaded with steel shot, as are required for shooting over wetlands in England and Wales, the plastic wads also protect the barrels from the abrasive effects of the shot. It is claimed that they improve patterns, though whether this is correct will depend on your definition of 'improvement'. They may well tighten up a pattern, both by holding the shot together and by restricting the numbers of flyers, but it is debateable whether this will increase or decrease the number of pheasants you kill. What they will do is litter up the ground in front of your peg, and they are practically impossible to gather up. However, most cartridge manufacturers still offer their wares loaded with the old-fashioned fibre wads, and unless you have some strong objection to using them they are a good, 'green' alternative to scattering plastic shot cups all over your shoot. In fairness to the cartridge manufacturers I should add that biodegradable versions of both cartridges and shot cups are being marketed as people become more aware of the need to protect the countryside and the public image of shooting sports.

It is worth experimenting with different brands and loads to find one that suits both your gun and your style of shooting. If you are really keen you could take yourself off to a pattern plate and conduct proper scientific experiments with different makes of cartridges, different loads and different shot sizes. Alternatively you may simply find

Note the spare cartridges in the left hand ready for an instant re-loading.

that you seem to shoot well with a particular brand and load. If so, then stick with that combination and tell yourself that you have discovered the right ammunition for your gun. A feeling of confidence goes a long way to producing the right results.

Don't be tempted to opt for magnum loads and high velocity propellants unless you have good reason for so doing. An extra quarter of an ounce of shot fired in the wrong direction will have no more effect on your quarry than a standard load aimed off target, but it may give you a nasty kick, particularly if you are using a light gun. The great majority of pheasants that escape the line of guns do so because they are cleanly missed: very few survive by flying through gaps in the pattern of an accurately aimed shot.

There is no such thing as the 'right' gun for pheasant shooting. Pheasants can offer the easiest or the most difficult shooting of all the game birds, and pheasant shots vary even more in their build and shooting styles. A logical case can be made for many different combinations of bore, choke and shot load: perhaps for increasing your chances of killing high birds; perhaps for ensuring that you will kill more of the birds that are within 'easy' range. In the end it all comes down to personal choice, and for most of us that choice is as likely to be influenced by the depth of our pockets and by aesthetic considerations as it is by a coldly logical calculation of what is most likely to put a pheasant into the game bag. We shoot for pleasure. If you believe that using a particular gun is going to make your shooting more enjoyable then you have all the reason you could possibly require to justify its purchase. I hope you will shoot well with it.

4

WHAT TO WEAR

The choice of what to wear for pheasant shooting has a lot in common with selecting a suitable gun for the task. As when selecting a gun most people are concerned with form as well as function, so when choosing shooting clothes most of us will be give a nod towards fashion as well as selecting clothes for reasons that are solely practical. In case that word 'fashion' has you visualising ruddy-faced countrymen in wellies and tweeds pirouetting along a catwalk, I should explain that 'fashion' in this context is more concerned with what is acceptable and conventional than in keeping up with the latest trends. In addition, as we saw in the previous chapter, there is no such thing as a universally 'right' gun for pheasant shooting and nor is there a standard 'right' uniform.

You can spend a great deal of money, if you have it to spare, or you can kit yourself out for a quite modest amount. There are no hard and fast rules, but there are conventions, and most shooting men tend to choose clothing that falls within the generally accepted limits. Where those limits lie will vary according to what kind of shoot you are attending and the company you are keeping. And of course, it is important that your clothes are functional: that they will keep you warm and dry as well as allowing you to swing your gun freely and that they will be tough enough to stand up to brambles, thorns and barbed wire fences if the type of shoot you frequent calls for a certain amount of cross country activity.

Pheasant shooting starts in October and continues through to the end of January. You might begin the season on a glorious autumn day, shooting in your shirtsleeves and end it standing in a drift and peering through icy swirls of snow as pheasants clatter through frozen branches as they try to get airborne. In between you are likely to have been soaked on some days and battered by gales on others as well as enjoying some of those crisp winter days when the sun shines, the rain stays away and the pheasants fly like angels through a clear blue sky. It is hardly reasonable to expect one set of clothes to meet all those eventualities.

Because pheasant shooting takes place mainly during November, December and January it is inevitable that some shooting days will be cold and wet. There is very little pleasure in standing shivering in a muddy puddle with rain trickling down your neck and water seeping through your boots, even when the very best of high pheasants are streaming over your peg. If you are stiff with cold and uncomfortably aware of frozen feet and soggy patches at your elbows, wrists and shoulders you are certainly not going

Beaters require tough, hard-wearing clothes to stand up to heavy cover.

to be on top shooting form, and unless you have dry clothes and a place to change into them, your drive home is going to be less than pleasant as well. Keeping the heat in and the rain out is probably the most important function of our shooting wardrobe.

Comfort and freedom of movement is also important. Pheasant shooting in particular calls for clothes that allow us a very free swing of the arms since at driven shoots, where the majority of pheasants are shot, the high bird is the norm and mounting the gun requires both arms to be lifted right above the head. A tight fitting coat that restricts the movement of arms and shoulders will provide an additional handicap that most of us simply don't need. Pockets should be wide enough for us to reach in and grab cartridges easily, even when our hands are cold and the cloth is stiff and wet. Waterproof over-trousers should be wide enough to put on without removing our boots or dancing a one-legged fandango while we try to ease them over the cleats on the soles. If climbing into waterproofs is too much of a sweat there is a tendency to put it off in the hope the rain will ease off – then, by the time we realise it has set in for the day, it is too late because we are soaked anyway.

Where you shoot will probably have a considerable influence on what you wear. Clothes that would be perfectly adequate for a mooch about the rough shoot with your spaniel might look badly out of place at a big, formal, driven shoot. The distinction between what is and what is not acceptable is not always clear, and indeed, is often not consistent. A brand new and extremely expensive jacket in one of the modern camouflage materials might draw some disapproving looks at that formal shoot, while another gun, dressed overall in what look like (and might well be) cast-offs from a charity shop would blend in perfectly. The fact that a coat is designed for field sports and is new, expensive and smart does not mean that it will be acceptable on every shoot.

Unfortunately there are no hard and fast rules to guide the novice: no guidelines to advise you where it is acceptable to turn out in jeans and an old sweater and where nothing less than a full tweed suit will do. It must also be borne in mind that it is not just the clothes that determine acceptability but also the body they are hanging from. If the Duke of Somewhereshire decides to go shooting in an army greatcoat held together with binder twine he will be regarded as amusingly eccentric. If you or I do it (I am assuming you are not of Royal blood) we will get, at the very least, some disapproving looks from our fellow guns.

How important the matter of being 'correctly' dressed will be also depends on your own personality. Some people feel uncomfortable if they don't look exactly 'right', while others are largely oblivious to what the rest of the world thinks of their appearance. There are also those individuals who set out to be different or controversial: who deliberately aim to surprise and shock. Which of these categories you fall into will obviously have a great deal to do with your choice of clothes – and not just for shooting.

Clothes make a statement about the wearer. I would surmise that for the majority of shooting people, who tend perhaps towards having fairly conservative natures, the impression they would like to give is of a quiet, conventional, competence that fits neatly in with the other guns on the shoot. This is not to say that there is no room for individualism and even eccentricity in our shooting clothes. The most conventional

A tweed coat, thick gloves, leggings and leather boots provide warmth on a cold day for this picker-up.

outfit can be given a lift by a fancy tie or a brightly coloured pair of socks. I seem to be seeing an ever wider selection of hats around shoots these days with the conventional flat caps and deerstalkers being supplemented by broad brimmed trilbys, Australian drover's hats and even the odd Stetson. They all add to the fun of the day and on a wet day a broad brimmed hat can be useful by keeping the rain off your glasses and out of your neck.

So what do you need to outfit yourself for pheasant shooting? Let us consider some of the choices available to you, their advantages and disadvantages, how much they are likely to cost and where you can buy them. Bear in mind that there *are* no rules, and that you could, if you were so minded, turn up in anything from pin stripes and a bowler hat to jeans and a tee shirt. Mind you, you might not get invited back again, though if you wore the bowler hat (but not the pin stripes) to the shoot at Holkham in Norfolk as you would probably be taken for one of the keepers, the original bowler having been designed by a previous owner of the estate to protect his keepers' heads from poachers wielding sticks and clubs.

Coats

The one item that you will require above all others is a warm, waterproof coat. The problem is that finding a coat that is genuinely water*proof* (as opposed to water *resistant*) is not as easy as it might seem from a casual perusal of the advertisements in the shooting press. Bear in mind that, on a rainy shooting day, you are likely to be out in the rain for five, six or even seven hours, and the coat that might keep you perfectly dry for twenty minutes while you nip down to the pub, or take the dog for a quick stroll, isn't necessarily going to keep repelling water for all that length of time. Mounting your gun strains the fabric at your elbows and across the shoulders, reaching into the pockets for cartridges allows rain to enter and seep through into the lining, and as the hours pass the little trickles that creep in at the neck mount up and soak your shoulders, back and chest.

A shooting coat should allow you plenty of room: both to add extra layers underneath on cold days and to give you freedom to swing your gun without constraint. Two good, big pockets on either side are useful to hold cartridges and should have flaps to close them to help keep the water out and keep the cartridges in when you are climbing fences or jumping ditches. If the flaps can be hooked up in the open position it will make reloading a little easier and the mouths of the pockets should be wide enough to allow your hand – and glove if you are wearing one – to reach in easily to grab cartridges and to emerge from the pocket when your fist is closed around the cartridges. Hand-warmer pockets are another useful feature of most coats designed for shooting, though they have a tendency to get waterlogged on wet days as water runs down your sleeves and into the pockets.

A high collar that you can turn up to protect your neck from the wind and the rain adds to your comfort and keeping it turned up is made simpler if there is an extra button or snap fastener to join the ends together under your chin. A hood can be a boon on wet days but it will restrict your vision on either flank as well as muffling sound. It is only when your hearing is restricted that you realise how much you rely on hearing the clatter of wings or the indignant squawk of a cock pheasant being flushed by a spaniel to alert you to the imminent likelihood of a shot. If your coat does have a hood it is helpful if it will fit over your cap, and of course you won't be able to use it if you are wearing a broad brimmed hat. A detachable hood that can be fixed on with snap fasteners when required allows you the widest choice of combinations of headgear and coat. Some hoods can be rolled up and tucked into a zipped compartment in the collar. This is a neat and tidy arrangement, but not ideal if you are caught in a sudden shower and would like to put your hood up quickly. By the time you have found the end of the zip, performed a short contortionist act trying to get your hands around the back of your neck and, finally, got the hood into position you will probably be soaked anyway.

The two coat materials most often seen in the shooting field are waxed cotton and tweed, though the modern 'wonder' fabrics that are claimed to keep you perfectly warm and dry while allowing your skin to breathe through the material are becoming more common. Loden cloth, a heavy felt like material is another natural material that has good thermal and water resistant properties. Waxed cotton coats – often referred to as 'Barbour' jackets even when they are manufactured by other firms – are as good as any of the alternatives at keeping the rain and wind out and are hard-wearing and long lasting as well as being universally acceptable: you will never look out of place in a conventional waxed jacket. They do need re-waxing from time to time if they are to retain their water resistance, and they have a tendency to get stiff in cold, wet weather. Largely impervious to thorns and brambles, they can still be ripped quite easily if you get caught on the barbed wire when you are crossing a fence. They also tend to make you very hot and sweaty on warm, damp days; something that tweed coats largely avoid as the material is much more 'breathable'.

Tweeds were the traditional choice of the country gentleman and still are in many cases. A good heavy tweed coat will keep you warmer than a waxed cotton one and will be almost as good at keeping the rain out. Wool will also keep you warm even when the cloth is soaking wet. The old Highlanders were said to dip their plaids in a burn on cold nights before wrapping themselves in them to sleep because wet wool supposedly kept them warmer than a dry plaid. I have never felt moved to try the experiment but there may well be truth in it and a wet tweed coat certainly doesn't feel as cold and clammy as a wet waxed cotton coat. Indeed, if you buy a tweed coat combined with one of the modern waterproof liners such as Goretex, it should keep you dry no matter how much rain falls on you. Even without a waterproof lining a good quality tweed will keep the rain out for a long, long time, though eventually the wet will get through, especially around the elbows and shoulders where the cloth is strained by movement. Note that the very light-weight tweed jackets sold for casual wear will neither resist thorns nor keep out the wet with anything like the efficiency of the heavier tweeds used to make proper sporting clothes.

The down side of tweed is that it soaks up rain rather than shedding it. This is an advantage in showery weather when compared with a waxed cotton coat that will tend to drip water onto your legs as it trickles down. On a day when the rain keeps on falling though, you will find your tweed coat getting heavier and heavier as the water builds up within the fabric. As long as you stay dry this isn't too much of a problem, but

A bright winter's day at a field trial. The gun wears tweed coat and plus twos, while the lady studying her programme has opted for a waxed cotton jacket.

beware of getting into your car while wearing the coat because all that water will leach out into the seat. It will also take a long time to dry out and possibly leave a sizeable puddle on your floor as it drips quietly away overnight.

Various modern, man-made fibres are used to make shooting coats and, if the advertising blurb is correct, will keep you warm and dry whatever the weather throws at you. If you are tempted to experiment with one of these you should question whether they will stand up to as much hard wear as tweed or waxed cotton. This may not be a problem if your shoot allows you to stand in the open at an easily accessible peg on every drive, but if you spend part of your time beating, or as a walking gun where cover has to be negotiated, the first bramble or thorn bush might just put a very expensive tear into your new coat.

Shooting coats – and jackets, breeks and trousers – tend to be made in generally subdued colours and patterns so that the wearer will blend in to the background and not cause the pheasants, partridges, grouse or whatever to swerve away when they spot him. I am not sure whether pheasants can see colours, though, given the flamboyant plumage of the cock pheasant, and the way they chase after my red van I suppose it is likely that they do. However: last Boxing Day one of the guns arrived, tastefully decked out in a bright red hat complete with Mickey Mouse style ears. I was

Shirt-sleeve order on the grouse moors at the start of the season but tweed breeks and waistcoats are still suitable even in the heat.

quite pleased to draw the peg next to him because I hoped the sight of the hat would cause the birds to swerve away and perhaps cross over my peg instead. Instead it almost seemed as if the pheasants were picking him out at a distance and then flying right over him. He killed more birds on the first drive than all the other guns combined.

That said, it is unlikely that the received wisdom of three centuries of sporting shooting is wrong, and I would strongly advise that you avoid bright colours when choosing a shooting coat. Some of the traditional tweed patterns may look quite flamboyant when seen up close but still blend in beautifully at a distance. Camouflaged clothing has become increasingly popular over the past few years and is available in a range of exotic patterns designed to render the wearer practically invisible. It is possible that this pattern of cloth might cause a few raised eyebrows on some of the more traditionally minded shoots, though I have never, personally, heard any objections voiced. If you are unsure then play safe and go for a traditional pattern.

Jackets

Particularly in the early part of the season you may find that the weather is too warm to require a heavy coat. A tweed jacket can be ideal for these days and for grouse and

Tweed cap, scarf, fleece and a modern, breathable jacket should keep this gun warm and dry whatever the weather.

partridge shooting, but unless you buy one made of really heavy cloth it is unlikely to get too much use later in the season. You can buy matching jackets and breeks to make up a proper shooting suit, and look very smart indeed, though on some shoots it is possible to overdo the smart element and become the subject of some gentle (or not so gentle) leg-pulling. I am not sure why a new jacket, new breeks or a new coat on their own will attract nothing more than a passing comment, while a new shooting suit will mark you out as ripe for ridicule, but it often seems to be the case. If you are a particularly sensitive soul then best proceed with caution where new suits are concerned.

That aside most of what I have said about coats will apply equally to jackets. The pockets are unlikely to be as capacious as those on a coat but in general a jacket will allow you easier access to your cartridge belt than when it is worn under a coat. Jackets tend to be cut a little tighter than coats, especially round the arms, so make sure you have freedom to swing your gun before buying.

Breeks

The majority of shooting men wear trousers that stop somewhere about the knees. This is not because of fashion, nor in order to save money on cloth, but because your legs from the knee down are liable to get wet and muddy and it is a lot easier to wash socks or replace them with a clean pair than to dry clean or wash full length trousers. There are three different styles to choose from: breeks, plus twos and plus fours. Breeks are the most common design and are cut to end just below knee level. Plus twos are cut several inches longer so that form a loose bag around the knees when they are fastened. Plus fours, beloved of the Edwardians and Victorians and worn for golf, fishing, shooting and just general out of town wear, are quite rare today but easily recognisable because the bag they form at the knees can droop down to almost mid-calf.

The exaggerated length of cloth used in plus fours probably owes more to Victorian fashion than to any practical reason but there is, nevertheless, a real benefit to be gained from having a somewhat loose fit around the knees. If your breeks are a tight fit at the knee the stretching effect on the cloth as you walk will encourage the rain to seep through on wet days. The loosely fitting cloth of the plus twos will keep the rain off your legs for much longer though when the rain persists for too long it will soak up water and end up as a soggy length of cloth flapping against the tops of your shins. The extra length of cloth used in plus twos also makes it easier to ensure that you don't develop an inch or two of bare skin between the end of the breeks and the top of your socks. While not exactly life threatening or liable to induce frostbite, the feeling of socks and breeks slipping apart can be surprisingly annoying. Plus twos, being longer and looser, are less prone to this particular minor aggravation.

Tweed is by far the most popular material for shooting breeks but you can also get them in moleskin, corduroy, Loden cloth and leather as well as in modern, man-made fibres. Whatever the material they will incorporate some means of securing them at the knees. This may be an elasticated cuff, a buckle, buttons, draw strings or a couple of strips of Velcro. Whatever it is you should ensure that it has enough margin of

Leather-faced breeks and a light jacket are this gun's choice for an autumn shoot.

adjustment for you to ensure that you can get a good, tight (but not circulation threatening) fit either over or under your socks depending on how you choose to wear them.

Boots

If you are to get the maximum enjoyment from your shooting it is essential to keep your feet warm and dry. Standing about for hour after hour with cold, wet feet will ruin your day, no matter how well the pheasants fly. Good boots are not cheap, but if you try to skimp on this most important item you will quickly discover that cheap boots are very rarely good. Footwear for the shooting man falls into three main categories that we will call shoes, boots and wellies.

The heavy, leather brogue type shoe is an excellent choice for the type of shoot where the extent of the guns' walking is limited to relatively short trips from vehicles to peg. A well made brogue is comfortable to walk in, will keep out the wet and will look smart, particularly when matched with a tweed suit and fancy shooting socks. Once the ground gets really muddy, or if any serious cross country walking is demanded, their limitations will show up and something more substantial will be required.

A leather boot, particularly if it incorporates a waterproof liner, is by far the best choice for practically all shooting days. The huge increase in popularity of hill walking has brought with it an enormous range of hiking boots, suitable for everything from parading about in a London park to staging an assault on Everest. Besides the vast choice of modern boots there are still traditional hill boots available, some designed for stalkers and shepherds and incorporating turned up toes and soles bristling with tacket nails and others hand built especially for the sportsman who combines good taste with extremely deep pockets.

There are several requirements for the ideal shooting boot. Above all, it should be comfortable: a snug, but not tight, fit when worn over the type of socks you will wear on a shooting day. The laces should give you a certain amount of leeway for those bitterly cold days when you might want to add an extra pair of socks or some insulated foot warmers. Boots that are too tight can be sheer torture by the end of a long day on your feet, but beware of over-compensating and ending up with boots that allow your feet to slide about inside them. Although you can add extra socks to fill the spare space you will find that the movement of your feet within the boots will quickly produce blisters.

Various lengths of boot are available from short ankle boots to those that reach almost up to the knees. If your shooting involves walking through boggy fields then the higher up the leg the better but otherwise this is largely a matter of personal preference and comfort. Leather is the traditional material for shooting boots, but there is quite a range of alternatives on the market and some boots are made from a combination of materials designed to add the flexibility and comfort of nylon or canvas type material from the ankle upwards to the robustness and hard wearing qualities of leather for the 'shoe' section.

The taller boots are usually fastened by laces that run through eyelets as far as the ankles then switch to open lugs for the rest of the way up the leg. These are much quicker and easier to lace and unlace than boots that have the laces running through eyelets right to the top of the leg. This may not be a problem when you are putting dry boots on first thing in the morning, but by evening, when the laces are soaked and caked with mud and your feet are cold, stiff and aching, it can be quite a job prising the boots off. This problem is compounded if you have to remove your boots at lunchtime to go inside to eat, then put them back on again afterwards while the keeper is tapping his watch and fretting because the birds will be starting to drift out of the coverts.

It goes without saying that the soles should have a good grip, whether this is a rubber tread or nailed leather. Some boots are advertised as having 'self-cleaning' treads, but I have never yet seen the boot that wouldn't collect a couple of pounds of clay when the owner walked it across a Suffolk plough. The tongue has to be sewn in right to the top of the boot if the boot is to be waterproof but make sure that there is still a wide enough gape to make it easy to get the boots on and off when your feet are cold and stiff as well as in the warmth and comfort of the shop.

Leather requires regular cleaning and polishing to keep it supple and smart. There are also various proprietary waxes and silicone sprays available to help keep the water out of your boots. Check the instructions before plastering your boots with wax because some of the breathable liners get clogged up and stop working if you use the wrong sort of treatment on them. Drying out leather boots by standing them in front of a fire or radiator is not a good idea as the leather can become cracked and brittle if the natural oils are removed. The modern, lightweight fibres may well be capable of standing more heat, but once again, check the instructions before you bung them in the oven.

The other standby for the shooting man's feet is, of course, the Wellington boot. The drawbacks of the wellie are well known: there is no ventilation so they make your feet sweaty, they are not the most comfortable things to wear if you are walking any distance, and in cold weather they let your feet freeze. Every pair of wellies I have owned has ended up leaking where the rubber flexes when I walk, but usually only after a few years' service. Add to that the fact that it is very easy to puncture a wellie with a thorn or to rip them when crossing a fence and it might appear that the wellie doesn't have very much going for it.

On the bright side though, a Wellington boot – provided you haven't put a hole through it – *will* keep out water even if you spend the whole day standing in a calf deep puddle. Even the best of waterproof leather is liable to succumb eventually under these conditions, but wellies are, quite simply waterproof. They are also easy to hose clean at the end of the day, quick to slip on and off and – provided you purchase a muted shade of green – completely classless. You can wear wellies to any shoot, anywhere and not attract a second glance. And if you do put a hole through them you can buy a tube of glue that will mend the hole and yet stay flexible enough not to crack as soon as you try walking again.

Nor are they expensive if you just want a pair of bog-standard boots. Equally, if you so desire you can pay an awful lot of money for wellies with a leather lining, designed to give you 'the comfort of a leather boot with the convenience of a Wellington'. The leather lining is undoubtedly comfortable but as to the claims that it allows your feet to breathe I am less certain. No matter what lining is incorporated the outside of a wellie boot is made of rubber, and rubber is just not a breathable fabric. A much more useful material used as a liner, in my opinion at least, is neoprene: the stuff used to make divers' wet suits. Having done a bit of diving I know from experience that a wet suit will keep you warm in water that is near freezing, and on really cold days it can transform the standard welly from an instrument of torture to a boot that is capable of keeping your feet warm as well as dry.

Hats

At the opposite end of your body you will require some form of headgear of which the flat cap, usually made from tweed, is the most common form. Apart from the obvious benefits of keeping off the rain and, on better days, keeping the sun out of your eyes and being a big help in keeping you warm a hat will also shield your face from the on-coming pheasants. A surprising amount of heat is lost through a bare head, particularly if you are somewhat under-endowed in the hair department. Ghillie hats and deerstalkers are also popular as are trilbys and some of the more exotic designs such as the drovers' hats and Stetsons mentioned earlier. Broad brimmed hats are great at keeping the rain off but they can be a liability once the wind gets up unless they incorporate some form of lanyard to keep them anchored in place. I heard a story of

Country fairs offer a wide choice of shooting clothes, often at bargain prices.

the host at a shoot whose hat blew off in the wind and rolled, like a cartwheel, right along the line of guns – every one of who saluted it with a shot, leaving it well ventilated but not much use in the rain.

Socks, Gloves, Ties and so on

If you are wearing breeks then long socks or stockings, will be essential to link the gap between trouser and boot. Wool is by far the best material for socks, though it has to be said that wool combined with a small proportion of artificial fibre will probably be harder wearing. Make sure that your socks are long enough to give you plenty of spare material to tuck under (or over) the ends of your breeks. Bright colours are generally acceptable if you want to make some sort of fashion statement and the really smart will keep their socks up with a pair of fancy garters with green tabs on the sides. The rest of us make do with ordinary elastic or a couple of bits of string. Incidentally, don't tie the strings too tight or you will cut off the circulation to your legs. If you decide to wear two pairs of socks, either to pad out your boots or to combat the cold, either make sure that both socks are long enough to be held up by your garters or wear the short pair on the outside and roll them down over the tops of your boots. If you wear a short pair of socks under a long pair the chances are that they will ruck up under your feet and cause considerable discomfort.

A variety of clothing on display from this happy team of guns.

Deciding whether to wear gloves or not can be a problem. Cold hands will do nothing to improve your shooting, but neither will it help if you are fumbling for the triggers in gloves that won't fit in the trigger guard. Proper shooting gloves made from thin leather will get over the latter problem but they won't do very much to combat the cold on a really icy morning. Lots of guns compromise by wearing a good, warm pair of gloves between drives but stuffing them in their pockets once the pheasants start flying. If your coat has hand warmer pockets – provided they are properly sited – you can hold your gun in the crook of your arm and stuff both hands in them while you are waiting for the next shot. If your are in such a busy spot that there is no time to tuck hands into pockets between shots you will probably not be noticing the cold anyway.

At the more formal shoots most guns will wear a tie. If you are shooting in a jacket as opposed to a coat a tie will round off the outfit properly and allow you to discreetly advertise your membership of BASC or the Game Conservancy if you so choose. On the practical side wearing a tie will help to keep the rain from trickling down your neck on wet days.

How many layers you wear under your coat will depend on how cold you anticipate the weather being on the day. Thermal underwear beneath your shirt and a sweater over the top can be supplemented by a fleece or a padded waistcoat when the temperature really plummets. A scarf can also make a considerable difference to your comfort as it will keep the rain out and your body heat in by sealing the gap around your coat collar. It is sensible to take along more than you think you will need. If there is no call for that extra sweater you can always take it off, but it will be no use to you on a cold day if it is sitting in a drawer back at home.

Waterproofs

Hopefully your coat will already be waterproof. Keeping your legs dry is another matter. Gaiters will keep your legs dry as far as the knees and are useful to prevent your socks getting snagged if you have to walk through brambles and thorns. There are some designs that incorporate a tight rubber seal around the boot that will enable you to cross water that is deeper than the tops of your boots without getting wet feet, though it is not advisable to linger too long. They will also keep your lower legs dry if you are walking up in sugar beet or turnips or shooting on a day when there is deep snow on the ground.

For serious rain or walking through kale or other high game cover you will need a pair of leggings. There are two kinds: those that are effectively waterproof trousers and those that are designed like chaps to cover the legs as far as the hemline of the coat. The latter are generally easier to put on when it starts to rain particularly if they can be opened out with snaps along the sides. They do have the disadvantage of offering no protection if you have to sit down on a wet seat, in the guns' trailer for example. For the gun who spends all his time standing at a peg the lightweight, nylon type of waterproof is adequate and has the advantage of being easily rolled up and stowed in gamebag or pocket. If you spend part of your shoot day as a beater you will need to choose something a lot more robust or it will not survive much exposure to thick cover.

Stout leggings are essential when you have to tackle long wet grass and rushes.

A third, and possibly better alternative to chaps or leggings, is the waterproof kilt: a length of waxed cotton that fastens around the waist like a skirt. One of these will shed water as effectively as a pair of leggings and, because there is no strain at the knees, will not allow the rain to seep through as leggings tend to do. Whether you are prepared to stand the smart remarks from your fellow guns is likely to be the main problem in choosing one of these.

Charity shops can be a useful source of shooting clothes, particularly for items like tweed jackets. You can save a considerable amount of money and attain that desirable look of an old campaigner at the same time. You can always pick up some bargains around the clothing stalls at Game Fairs: indeed, there are times when you may wonder how anyone could possibly sell a coat so cheaply and still make a profit. One stall will sell you a tweed coat for £40: another will relieve you of more than £400 for something that doesn't look a whole lot different. The choice – and the risk – is yours. It is perhaps worth saying that, while the £40 coat may not last as long as the £400 model you could buy another nine for the same outlay.

Shooting clothes are not exactly a uniform, but most of us prefer to look the part rather than wearing clothes that mark us as an outsider to the sport. The main thing about whatever you wear is that it keeps you warm and dry while allowing you the freedom to shoot. If it is also hard wearing and looks right – not too smart, not too scruffy – then you are pretty well equipped for the job.

5 ACCESSORIES

If you take the time to flip through the pages of a shooting magazine, particularly around Christmas time, you will find a bewildering variety of shooting accessories advertised, all designed to make your shooting day a better, more enjoyable experience. Most of them will be more or less useful at some time in your shooting career, and some of them may even come close to meeting the advertisers' claims. Some offer the shooting man an expensive taste of unashamed luxury, though whether such extravagance will actually make your shooting more accurate or otherwise increase your enjoyment of the day is open to debate. Will you really have a more enjoyable day after drawing a sterling silver peg finder rather than one made from plastic or improvising with eight slips of paper, folded in a hat?

Once you have your gun, some cartridges and suitable clothes to wear there is nothing – absolutely nothing – else that is essential to kit you out for a day pheasant shooting. There are one or two items that most guns would automatically include in their kit but none that are actually vital. Let us try to sort through the delights on offer and distinguish the things that you need from those that are simply nice to have on hand and the odd ones that are best avoided altogether.

Head of the list of the latter is the mobile phone. Leave it at home or in the car. If you are so attached to it that you can't bear to be parted from it then at least switch it off. You are here to shoot; not to consult your stockbroker, bookmaker, secretary, mistress, restaurant proprietor or anyone else. I once saw a gun on our syndicate shoot get so wrapped up in a conversation on his mobile that he forgot to get his gun out of the slip. The first two pheasants of the drive went right over him while he struggled to switch off the phone and get the gun ready for action. He failed: and just to prove that there is a God, those were the only two pheasants to go anywhere near him on that drive. I haven't seen him using a mobile during a drive since then.

You can probably manage quite adequately without designer sunglasses, a specially made, zip fastening canvas bag to hold your wellies and a palm pilot computer to calculate your kills to cartridges ratio. Leaving those aside though, what are the accessories that most shooting men would consider useful, if not actually essential? A lot will depend on what type of pheasant shoot you frequent. Driven shoots where there are beaters, pickers up and a game cart to carry away the fallen birds will make less demands on the guns than those where you are involved in beating as well as

A cartridge belt worn outside the coat gives instant access for quick re-loading.

shooting, have to take a turn as a walking gun and are expected to collect and carry any game you shoot.

Cartridge Belts and Bags

You can carry your cartridges in your coat pocket. Many guns find that this is the easiest arrangement for having cartridges on hand for reloading. If you are only expecting a dozen or so shots then a pocketful of cartridges is adequate and you might as well carry them that way as any other. If you anticipate the chance of more than

Transferring cartridges from belt to pocket ready for the next drive.

just a few shots though you will need something other than your pockets to carry your ammunition. The choice is between a cartridge bag and a cartridge belt. You may well decide you need both.

The standard cartridge belt, made from leather or canvas, usually fitted with twenty-five loops provides an easy way of carrying spare cartridges in a reasonably accessible manner. Twenty-five cartridges dumped into a coat pocket drag your coat down with their weight, whereas the same number of cartridges worn around the waist in a cartridge belt will be barely perceptible. It is important that the loops hold the cartridges tightly enough to prevent them slipping out, though not so tightly that

A cartridge bag rather than a belt is the choice for this gun.

they are not easily removable when your fingers are stiff with cold or wrapped up in gloves. Some belts are made with metal or plastic clips rather than loops so that the cartridges can be broken out a fraction faster than from a conventional belt. This may be something that you would find useful if your shoot sends birds over you in sufficient quantities to require speed loading, but beware of scratching the butt of your gun against the metal clips if you are wearing the belt outside your coat.

It is useful to have a belt that has a long tongue with sufficient holes so that you can wear it either outside or inside your coat. Outside gives you instant access to your cartridges but it also exposes them to the wet. If they are inside you may find yourself fumbling with zips and buttons just as the best pheasant of the day sails over your head. I compromise by wearing my cartridge belt under my jacket but keeping a few cartridges in my pocket ready for use, and topping them up from the belt between flushes.

The alternative to a cartridge belt is a leather or canvas cartridge bag. This is usually provided with a shoulder strap, but they are also available attached to a belt to wear around your waist. In effect the cartridge bag acts like an external pocket. Bags come in various sizes to hold anything from twenty or thirty cartridges up to a hundred and more. The bag should have a good, wide gape and a flap that can be folded back out of the way to allow you to reach in a grab cartridges easily when you need to reload in a hurry. The shoulder strap or belt needs to be broad, especially if you have one of the larger bags. A hundred cartridges will weigh eight to ten pounds and a narrow strap will soon cut a groove into your shoulder.

The logical way to use a cartridge bag is to adjust the strap so that it hangs at the right height to be easily available to your hand when you are reloading. However: many guns use their bag as a magazine rather than loading directly from it, storing cartridges for immediate use in their pockets and replenishing them from the bag as necessary. If you do work this way, and have the bag lying on the ground in front of you as most of us do, remember that it is not a good idea to employ it as a temporary dog tether.

Security Cabinets

A condition of holding a shotgun certificate is that the gun must be stored securely when not in use. Although the law does not actually specify that your guns must be stored in a steel cabinet most, if not all, police forces will require you to have one before they will issue you with a shotgun certificate. The days when you could hang your shotgun over the fireplace or keep it propped up behind the kitchen door are long past.

A basic security cabinet suitable for four shotguns, made of steel and equipped with two good locks can be obtained for around £100 and probably less if you find one for sale second-hand. Alternatively, if your taste and your wallet allows you can spend several thousand pounds on a security cabinet disguised as a bookcase or chest of drawers. Whatever your selection it should be fixed solidly to an internal wall using rag bolts and preferably located so that it is out of sight from windows. A determined thief with time and a crowbar could probably still make off with the cabinet complete with

Off to the next drive, complete with shooting stick, canvas gun slip and a waterproof hat.

contents to open at his leisure, but a standard steel cabinet will defeat the casual burglar. Other arrangements, using steel chains through trigger guards may be acceptable in some areas but in general you will have to have a proper cabinet. It is a one off expense and certainly worth while if it saves your guns from a burglar. You can also use it to store other valuable household items in relative safety.

Gun Slips

When I first started shooting we carried our guns over our arms from the moment we left the house until we returned at the end of the day. Once you had invested ten shillings in a gun licence you could wander along the streets quite happily with your gun on open display, provided of course that it wasn't actually loaded. Today you would probably cause a panic among the general public and end up being arrested. A gun slip – or some other form of gun cover – is an almost essential part of the shooting man's equipment.

A gun slip will offer a fair amount of protection from knocks and scratches when you are travelling in a crowded trailer. Gun barrels can be dented surprisingly easily and are not cheap to repair, nor is it desirable to have a wet Labrador trample mud into the engraving. For safety reasons many shoots insist that all guns are kept in a slip at all times apart from when the owner is standing at a peg and a slip will also keep your gun out of the rain and snow on wet days.

The simplest and cheapest gun slips are made of plain, unlined canvas or nylon. Slightly better versions will be lined with sheepskin or a man-made equivalent and offer considerably more protection from bumps and scratches. Better still, but priced accordingly, are those made from solid leather. I note that some magazines offer slips in camouflage colours. There may be sound reasoning behind this but I must confess that it escapes me. If you have dropped your gun slip down somewhere near your peg the last thing you need is for it to blend in with the background and make itself difficult to find. If you are deer stalking and expecting a shot your rifle is hardly going to be wrapped up in its cover. I suppose there might be a case for the stalker who has to carry his gun slip with him, but for the pheasant shot a simple slip made of plain canvas or leather is more than adequate.

Gun Cases

A gun case is not actually essential. You can transport your gun to and from the shoot wrapped up in your gun slip, and between times it will be locked in the security cabinet. However, if your gun comes complete with its own case, or if you can pick one up at auction or second-hand it will provide a rather more robust travel pack than a slip. The best guns are usually supplied in oak and leather cases, lined with velvet and complete with snap caps, oil bottles, cleaning rods and other useful items such as turn screws and chamber brushes.

Sometimes the case alone will cost far more than most of us spend on a gun. As well as the normal box-shaped cases you will also come across solid leather 'leg of mutton' cases, so called because of their shape. These too offer good protection for your gun while in transit and can sometimes be picked up quite cheaply. A more modern alternative to the traditional oak and leather case is the foam lined aluminium case: particularly useful if you travel by air and have to consign your gun to the cargo hold.

Ear Defenders

Ear defenders are considered essential by some and totally unnecessary by others. It is a fact that the report of a shotgun is loud enough to damage your hearing – permanently. Gun deafness is not a temporary problem. Once gone your hearing is gone forever. It is therefore sensible to wear some form of hearing protection when shooting, though I must confess that I never have and as far as I can tell my hearing is still okay. You can get ear defenders made either as inserts that go into the ear canal or as headphones that fit over the ears themselves. The cheapest are simply physical barriers to the noise of the gun firing and will also deaden all other sounds, while the more expensive are supposed to allow you to hear normal noises while protecting you from the report of the gun being fired. In a clear case of don't do as I do: do as I say, I would advise anyone taking up shooting to equip themselves with ear defenders and

A game bag or game carrier would leave this gun's hands free for the next shot.

use them right from the start. Some people shoot all their lives with no protection and no hearing difficulties, but others suffer serious damage from just a few shots.

Game Bags and Game Carriers

If the only time you have to carry the birds you shoot is when you collect them from around your peg and take them across to the game cart you can manage perfectly well by just holding them around their necks or by their legs. By the time you start picking up the fallen birds the drive will be over and your gun should be safely back in its gun slip. If you are walking up with your dogs or are taking a turn as a walking gun on a driven shoot and need to carry any shot game then a game bag or carrier will make your job a lot easier.

Game bags are normally equipped with a net on the outside so that shot game can be allowed to cool as it is carried, and a waterproof lining of some sort so that any blood or other contamination can be washed out at the end of the day. Make sure that your bag has a good, broad strap. Half a dozen pheasants are surprisingly heavy and will soon wear a groove in your shoulder if the strap is too narrow. Game bags come

A traditional version of the game cart.

in various shapes and sizes from a simple canvas carry all to those equipped with spare pockets and divided into two or three waterproof compartments. If you are going to use the bag for walked up shooting the extra compartments are useful to carry your waterproofs, lunch, spare cartridges, first aid kit, thermos flask and whatever else you need to take along. If all you need is a bag to carry dead game the simplest design will suffice.

The bigger the bag the more pheasants it will hold. This may or may nor be a good thing. If you are shooting on your own then you obviously need enough capacity to carry everything you expect to shoot. On the other hand, if there are half a dozen of you shooting and you are the only one with a game bag…. There are times when size certainly does matter, and being the one with the biggest game bag is definitely not an advantage.

A game carrier made from two loops of stiff wire joined by a broad strap and designed so that you can slide pheasants' heads into the loops is a handy alternative to the game bag. You can carry it folded up in your pocket or stuffed down the side of your boot so that it is out of the way until you need it. An alternative design has leather loops that fasten to your belt and can be noosed around the necks of your shot birds. Both have an advantage over the conventional game bag in that they are completely unobtrusive until needed, though obviously they are useful only for carrying shot game and can't be used for your lunch etc. A bag also offers some protection for your clothes: game carriers tend to allow blood to drip down onto your jacket and breeks.

Shooting Sticks

A shooting stick is not so much a stick as a mobile seat. If you find that standing at a peg is hard on your knees or hips then a shooting stick is an excellent investment allowing you to take the weight off your joints between shots but allowing you to rise easily when a pheasant comes over your peg. They are also useful when visiting game fairs, point to points, agricultural shows and the like, doubling up as a walking stick and a seat. Some even come equipped with umbrellas, though in the event of a shower you have to choose between comfort and dryness. I suspect that opening a brightly coloured umbrella in the middle of a drive might not be too popular with the keeper or the shoot captain.

Sticks in General

A stick, whether it is topped with a lovingly crafted shepherd's crook or is just a length of hazel cut from the hedge, is both useful and, at times, a nuisance to the shooting man. Used for its prime function as a walking stick it will be invaluable on steep, slippery slopes, when plodding through wet plough or to gauge the depth of a stream before venturing a foot. It can be used to tether a wayward dog, to rattle the undergrowth and tap trees when beating, to finish off a wounded pheasant, to point out some distant feature of interest to your fellow guns and to lean on between times. Then there are the times when you are walking up expecting a shot and have the stick in one hand and the gun in the other and have to drop the stick every time a bird gets up, then go back and retrieve it after the shot. Most guns seem to carry a stick when out shooting. All designs are acceptable from the most elaborately carved to the simple thumb stick. All can be broken if employed too vigorously in the beating line. When this happens the simple stick cut from the hedge is at a distinct advantage as regards replacement cost.

Cleaning Kits

You will need a cleaning kit for your gun unless it is to rust away inside and out. Modern cartridges are much less corrosive to barrels than they were fifty years ago when practically every gun in use in our village was more or less pitted with rust. It was not unusual to see guns 'repaired' with lumps of brazing metal where a hole had appeared in a barrel. Proper cleaning, every time the gun is used, will prevent this and should ensure that your gun will last your entire lifetime if you so desire.

You can clean your gun quite satisfactorily with nothing more than a cleaning rod, some toilet paper, a can of oil, a soft cloth and an old toothbrush. You can also, if you prefer, spend several hundred pounds on a cleaning kit housed in an oak case containing an ebony cleaning rod, silver oil bottles and, for all I know, gold backed brushes. Between the two extremes you will almost certainly find a kit to suit you both in the matter of contents and price. The quality of the kit is of far less importance than making sure that you use it, properly and thoroughly every time you go shooting.

Priests and Dispatchers

It is an unfortunate fact that every shot fired at a pheasant will not result in either a clean miss or an instant kill. It is inevitable that you will, from time to time, find yourself with a wounded pheasant in your hands and the need to dispatch it quickly and efficiently. Some guns cultivate the knack of breaking the neck with a swift flick of the wrist but this spoils the look of the carcase when birds are braced up and hung in the game cart. A better and quicker alternative is a sharp blow to the back of the head. If you carry a walking stick it is possible to use this to administer the blow, but because of the length of the stick this is not particularly easy and you are quite likely to end up with sore knuckles on the hand that is holding the bird. A fisherman's priest: a short club, often with a bit of lead in the end to add weight, can be carried in the pocket ready for use and will do the job with the minimum of fuss.

There are also patent bird dispatchers on the market, usually in the form of special pliers that either dislocate the neck or crush the brain. Never be tempted to improvise by knocking the pheasant's head against the barrel of your gun: the blood that gets spattered on the barrels will lift the finish and rust the metal underneath almost as efficiently as if you had sprayed them with acid.

Knives

A few years ago every countryman and country boy carried a pocket-knife as a matter of course. Boy scouts wore sheath knives as a part of their uniform. Nowadays you are

Examining a pair of binoculars: trade stands at game fairs offer a wide range of shooting accessories.

liable to be arrested for carrying a knife unless you can show good reason for being in possession of it. A shoot day offers a variety of possible good reasons: cutting strings to brace up the birds, hocking a rabbit so that it can be hung from a pole, cutting a stick from the hedge for beating or simply peeling your lunch-time apple. If it incorporates corkscrew, screwdriver, nail scissors, tooth pick, leather punch and one of those things for getting stones out of horses' hooves then so much the better!

Position Finders

It is usual to draw for places at the start of a driven shoot. Once each gun has drawn his number and established whether the shoot numbers from the right or from the left and how many they move up between drives, his place at each drive is established and no suspicions of favouritism should then cloud the day. Some shoots are less democratic and allow places to be allocated by the host or the shoot captain. Where there is a draw though it is necessary that some form of position finding device is employed. The simplest method is to write the numbers down and draw them from a hat, or to use playing cards. Usually though someone in the shoot will have a set of position finders and these will be used to sort the guns out before the first drive.

In its simplest form the position finder is a small leather wallet with pockets stitched for each of eight or ten plastic, ebony, silver, platinum or no doubt, if you are prepared to pay for them, solid gold, numbered sticks. The sticks are slipped into the wallet with the numbers hidden: you draw one at random and replace it with the number showing so that it is not drawn twice. All that is required of you then is that you remember the number you have drawn and correctly calculate your position at each subsequent drive. In passing, I might say that this is a procedure that occasionally seems to baffle some otherwise extremely intelligent men.

Other types of position finder are available. Some shoots kick off the day by offering the guns a shot of sloe gin or something similar in small silver cups, each cup having a peg number inscribed on the base and invisible until the cup has been drained. This seems like a convivial way to begin the day, provided that the cups and the measures of alcohol are not too large. The best organised shoots sometimes present each gun with a card which, depending on the number he has drawn, will indicate his peg number at every drive. Then all the gun has to do is to remember what he has done with the card. And which drive he is on. Unless you are the host or the shoot captain you are unlikely to *need* a set of position finders, but they do make a very acceptable Christmas present and you never know: one day the shoot captain may have left his in his other coat and you can step in to save the day. Or at least, to save someone the bother of numbering eight slips of paper and calling for a hat.

Hand Warmers

Again, not strictly necessary, but at times a very useful addition to the shooting man's kit, is the hand warmer. These are little devices that are kept in the pockets and give off heat when activated, and a real comfort they can be on cold, wet days. Some consist of a fuel rod burning – smouldering is a better term – inside a metal box while others employ a chemical reaction and are activated by squeezing them. If you find it difficult to shoot while wearing gloves a set of hand warmers could make all the difference to your enjoyment of your shooting in the depths of winter.

Hip Flasks

Lots of guns carry a hip flask, and a nip from the flask can add a little glow of internal warmth even if medical opinion tells us that alcohol is not a sensible way to combat the cold. It is generally considered good manners to offer the flask around for your companions to have a nip, and of course, those of your companions who have flasks of their own will almost certainly return your hospitality. And therein lies a possible problem.

At risk of sounding Puritanical, it must be said that alcohol and firearms are not the best of company. A nip from the flask between drives, a glass of wine over lunch and perhaps a port to round off the meal are an integral part of the day on many shoots and add to the overall pleasure of the day – provided that they are kept within sensible limits. A 'sensible limit' will not be the same for everyone, so don't be tempted to try and match some beetroot-nosed Colonel dram for dram throughout the day. Enough said.

The flask itself can come in a variety of materials and prices, from a simple pewter receptacle to something in beautifully chased sterling silver. The contents can vary almost as much and may come as a shock to the system if you take too hearty a sip

Something to warm the guns between drives: most people settle for a hip flask rather than the whole bottle.

at someone's special mixture only to discover that it tastes like rotgut whisky blended with disinfectant. Sloe gin, a decent malt whisky, ordinary whisky mixed with ginger wine, Drambuie or cherry brandy are common flask fillers. You may prefer something different. If it is too exotic I would prefer a warning when you offer it to me. A decent, single malt is always acceptable of course.

Game Books

Finally, one thing that may bring a lot of retrospective pleasure, is a game book. It doesn't take long to make a few notes once you are back home, warm and dry with the dog fed and the gun cleaned. Include the date, the location, who was there, what the weather was like, the total bag and whatever was memorable about the day. If you are concerned about such matters you can add how many cartridges you fired and how many birds you killed plus, if someone was operating one of those infernal clickers, how well the guns did as a unit. In years to come you will bring back a lot of happy memories just by leafing through your game book and remembering days that would otherwise be long forgotten.

A game book is similar to most of the other shooting accessories we have considered in that you can spend as much or as little as you like on it. A simple school notebook costing a few pence from the stationers will suffice, or you can commission a leather bound volume inscribed with your initials and filled with pages of finest vellum. In the end the real pleasure of shooting comes from what we do on the day, but there is also a certain amount of satisfaction to be gleaned from having good quality extras – 'big boys' toys' as they are sometimes described – to complement it. Like the CD player, the satellite navigation and the air conditioning in our car, they won't make that much difference to the journey, but they do help to make it more enjoyable.

6

DOGS

Some guns go right through their shooting life without ever owning a dog. Indeed, it can be argued that, for the gun who does all his shooting at formal driven shoots where beaters and pickers up are employed with their dogs to get live birds into the air and to collect the dead and wounded once they have been over the guns, there is no need for the guns themselves to have dogs. Some keepers and shoot captains would go further and maintain that guns' dogs are nothing more than a damned nuisance – and for some guns and some dogs there may be a grain of truth in the assertion.

But not all pheasant shoots employ professional pickers up and beaters. Not all guns do all their shooting standing at a peg and waiting for birds to be driven over them. Some shoots are totally reliant on their guns' dogs to flush live birds and recover dead ones. Some syndicates make it a condition of membership that a gun has a good (or even a not so good) dog. And many guns, myself included, would rather leave the gun at home and work the dog than leave the dog at home and use the gun.

Whole books are written about training and working gundogs: indeed, whole books are written about training and working individual breeds. In a single chapter we can only take the briefest glance at dogs for pheasant shooting: an overview with perhaps enough hints to guide you towards the right choice of dog for your own particular shoot and the right way to work him once you have got him. There is no doubt that a good dog can contribute enormously to the pleasure you get from shooting, though it must also be said that bad dog can be a sore trial for his owner and at times an even worse trial for the rest of the guns. For the most committed of trainers the dog can become the reason for shooting in itself: in other words, they go shooting because of the pleasure they get from working their dogs rather than working a dog because it adds to the pleasure they get from shooting. Many of us start off in the latter category and find ourselves sliding gradually into the former until our dogs effectively take over our lives. Be warned!

The Gundog Breeds

It is not my intention to look in detail at all of the different breeds of gundog that are available to the pheasant shooting man. There are something like twenty-five or thirty recognised gundog breeds in Britain today, plus deliberate crosses such as sprockers and droppers and the non-gundog breeds that turn up on shoots from time to time and in many cases do an excellent job. There was a rough collie that used to beat and pick up at a shoot in which I had an interest and it was better at its job than many of the specialist gundogs. I have shot grouse over a Border terrier, and pheasants flushed by a lurcher and the beating line at our little syndicate usually includes two or three Jack Russell terriers. A lack of space suggests however that we confine our look at gundogs to the more mainstream canine varieties.

Dogs fulfil two main functions on shoots. We use them to find live game and flush it so that it can be shot, and we use them to retrieve dead or wounded game. In many cases we want our dog to do both jobs: find and flush the bird first and then retrieve it after we have shot it. Life can be confusing for a dog, especially if he is expected to work as a retriever on one drive and a beating dog on the next as is the case with many small syndicates. It takes a very good dog (generally under the influence of a very good trainer/handler) to cope with the heady excitement of going out and rattling through a covert pushing birds out and getting them on the wing at one drive and then to sit patiently while pheasants are falling all around him at the next.

Gundogs are classified in four groups: the Retrievers, the Spaniels, the Pointers and Setters and the Hunt, Point and Retrieve breeds. Of these it is the first two groupings that are of most interest to the pheasant shot, though the various pointing breeds are sometimes used in rough shooting and in the beating line. If you can persuade a

A mixed bunch of Labradors and Springers ready to take their place in the beating line.

Pointer or an Irish setter to sit patiently by your side while you shoot driven pheasants then you are either a very talented trainer or you have an unnaturally calm dog. Some of the HPR breeds are claimed to be all round shooting dogs, but unless you have a over-riding reason for choosing something other than a spaniel or a retriever as a pheasant shooting dog you will almost certainly be best to stick with conventional wisdom and make your choice from one of these groups.

The Retrievers

The three most commonly encountered retrieving breeds in Britain are the **Labrador**, Golden and Flatcoated Retrievers, plus the occasional Chesapeake Bay, Curlycoated and Nova Scotia Duck Tolling Retrievers. Of these the Labrador is by far and away the most popular of the retrieving breeds and it is a rare shoot that will not have its quota of Labs taking part. Generally reasonably placid by nature, the working Labrador often doubles as household pet. Their short, dense coat makes them largely impervious to cold and wet, and most Labs like nothing better than to hurl themselves in to water in pursuit of a retrieve. The short coat also limits the amount of mud, muck, burrs, briars and twigs that will be picked up in the course of a working day: something that can be a problem with the longer coated **Golden Retriever**.

The Golden Retriever, with its gentle, friendly and quiet nature makes a good family

The black Labrador is the most popular of all the gundog breeds.

pet as well as a working dog. The dogs my family kept in the 1950s had short, thick coats of a reddish gold colour, but most of those I see today have very heavy coats that are almost white: a result of breeding specifically for the show ring. As with all gun dogs it is important that you ensure that your Golden comes from working stock if you intend to use him in the shooting field. Goldens are generally quite placid but can be very stubborn and show great perseverance when on the scent of wounded birds.

The **Flatcoated Retriever**, in contrast to the general run of Labradors and Goldens, has a lively, happy-go-lucky temperament that reflects the influence of the setter breeds on his ancestry. A bigger but less heavily built dog than the Labrador with a longer coat and feathering on the legs and tail, the Flatcoat was by far the most popular of the retrieving breeds at the end of the nineteenth century: a position that has since been usurped by the Labrador. They are said to be slower to mature than the other retrieving breeds, but a well-trained and properly controlled Flatcoat is a pleasure to watch with its obvious joy in its work.

The other breeds all have their devotees, but are comparatively rarely seen working on shoots. The Curlycoated Retriever was once more popular but has been in decline as a working dog for many years, whereas the Chesapeake Bay and Nova Scotia Duck Tolling Retrievers have been recently introduced from their native countries and may well begin to be seen more often on shoots in the future.

Golden Retrievers with the guns at the start of the shooting day.

The Spaniels

There are seven breeds of spaniel to choose from, though one of them, the Irish Water Spaniel has more in common with the retrievers than with the rest of the spaniel breeds. The two most popular spaniels, by a very large margin, are the English Springer and the Cocker and probably ninety-five per cent of working spaniels are one or other of these breeds or a cross between the two known as a 'Sprocker'. The other spaniel breeds, sometimes referred to as the 'minor breeds' are the Welsh Springer, the Sussex, the Field, the Clumber and the previously mentioned Irish Water Spaniel.

The spaniel you are most likely to see working on your shoot is the **English Springer Spaniel**. Spaniels were being used as sporting dogs long before retrievers were introduced, flushing game for falconers even before the advent of shooting as a sport. The Springer is at his best when hunting for game, questing through cover and pushing out birds for the guns to shoot. They are also accomplished retrievers and are quite capable of sitting beside a gun during a drive, watching and marking each pheasant as it is shot. Whether they will do this with quite the same stolid patience as a Labrador is open to question. It is unlikely that you will ever persuade the little **Cocker Spaniel** to display patience of this level. Eager, inquisitive, excitable and sometimes downright wilful, the Cocker is not the dog for the man who wants a quiet,

The 'Sprocker' is a cross between a Springer and a Cocker Spaniel.

The English Springer Spaniel.

uneventful life. On the other hand, the sight of a Cocker rattling through cover, bursting with joys of the hunt can lift the spirits on the dullest of days.

Cockers and Springers share common ancestors: indeed, at the end of the nineteenth century they were distinguished according to their weight and it was possible to produce both Springers and Cockers from the same litter. Both breeds are sharply divided between show and working strains and it is worth stressing once again that it is absolutely essential that you select your dog from proper working stock if he is ever to be of any use as a gundog. Cockers are quite a bit smaller than Springers and thus not quite so well equipped to deal with a long succession of retrieves on heavy game like pheasants, though they give nothing away when it comes to finding and flushing live birds. In between the two breeds as far as size goes is the **Welsh Springer** – much less common than either the English Springer or the Cocker but still maintaining a presence on quite a lot of shoots.

The other minor breeds are rarely seen out shooting, though there are still working kennels of Clumbers, Field, Sussex and Irish Water Spaniels. The **Clumber** is a much heavier and slower breed than the other spaniels but can make a good, steady rough shooting dog as well as a useful retriever with the temperament to sit patiently at a peg. The **Irish Water Spaniel** is built more like a retriever than a spaniel, with relatively long legs and a thick, curly coat. Working owners say they make excellent, all-round gun dogs with a particular propensity for retrieving from water.

Cocker Spaniels are great fun to work with their boundless enthusiasm and independent nature.

The Pointing Breeds

We can consider all the pointing breeds together since they are not generally the right choice for pheasants other than for the gun whose interest is confined to rough shooting. A pointing dog, whether he is one of the 'British' breeds that were bred to specialise on grouse and partridge, or from 'continental' stock: the Hunt, Point and Retrieve breeds that are classed as all round gundogs, is bred for a specific purpose: *to find game and point it*, holding the point until the guns have come up and positioned themselves in readiness for the shot.

The original reason for having dogs that would point was to allow a falcon to gain height before flushing its quarry, or to allow a net to be drawn over a tightly clapped covey. In more recent times the pointing instinct meant that dogs could be encouraged to roam well out of gunshot because when they found game they would point it rather than flush it, thus allowing a much larger area of ground to be covered than if the dog always had to stay with thirty yards or so of the guns.

Pointing breeds are ideal if you are walking up your quarry, alone or with just one other gun. They are of limited use as beaters' dogs, not because they won't find pheasants, but because they are liable to come on point in thick cover and be difficult to find. In addition, once the other dogs in the beating line realise what a point implies they will quickly become adept at nipping in and flushing the birds – a practice that is

German Shorthaired Pointer complete with luminous collar to help his owner spot him when he points.

almost guaranteed to make your pointing dog unsteady. It is also worth noting that pheasants, with their propensity to run rather than crouch in cover, are not the ideal quarry for the pointing breeds. That said, you can have a lot of fun shooting pheasants over pointing dogs, though you may need to be pretty slick getting to the point and working it out.

The 'British' breeds: Pointers, Irish, English and Gordon Setters: are really more at home on the grouse moors or working partridges in stubbles and roots than they are on a pheasant shoot. The 'continental' breeds: German Shorthaired and Wirehaired Pointers, Weimaraners, Hungarian Vizslas, Italian Spinones, Large and Small Munsterlanders, Brittany Spaniels and the like are all bred to retrieve as well as to hunt for game, and can all offer good sport to the rough shooter. In general though, the pheasant shooter is likely to be best served by a retriever or a spaniel rather than one of the pointing breeds.

The Role of the Dog

Gundogs have two distinct roles: flushing and retrieving. If you are walking up, the two happen almost simultaneously: the dog flushes a pheasant, you shoot it and then send the dog to make the retrieve – assuming that the dog isn't already on the way. At a driven shoot the two roles are usually separated. One group of dogs will be working in the beating line, hunting out the birds from cover and pressing them until they take flight. Despite his bright colours a cock pheasant can become almost invisible when he crouches down in the tiniest scrap of cover, and a hen can vanish just by squatting motionless on practically bare ground. The beating dog must therefore investigate every bit of cover using his nose to sniff out the scent of the hidden pheasants. Some

A cock pheasant brought to hand on a frosty morning.

pheasants take off directly from where they have been hiding but others will run, sometimes for quite a distance and at a surprising speed until they are forced into the air.

How active the beating dog is required to be will depend very much on the number of pheasants in the covert. At a big shoot where the bag will be two or three hundred birds and each drive will hold several hundred pheasants it is likely that the keeper will want the beaters' dogs, if they have dogs at all, to be kept very strictly under control while the birds are quietly shepherded to a flushing point and then gently encouraged to take flight a few at a time. A wild dog that charges in among them and flushes several hundred at once will not be invited again. It doesn't matter if a couple of dozen pheasants manage to slip back through the beating line, or crouch unseen beneath cover. Plenty more will go over the guns. If however the day's bag is expected to be more modest, and each wood likely to hold only a few birds the emphasis will be on finding every single pheasant, if at all possible, and as long as the dogs are hunting and getting birds on the wing it probably won't matter too much how eager – some might say wild – they are in their approach. (This is not to say that the gun who shoots in a small syndicate should be content with a dog that is undisciplined and out of control. A properly trained dog, quartering its ground methodically will always find more birds than one that flies around a wood in a frenzy of uncontrolled excitement.)

Pheasants will often start to run ahead of the beaters as soon as they hear them entering the wood and their foot scent provides an obvious temptation for the dogs to get their noses onto a line and track an individual bird while leaving the bulk of the cover un-hunted. Ideally, a beating dog will quarter the ground in front of his handler and ignore the foot scent of running birds that have legged it away to the far end of the wood. Birds that sit tightly under cover should be pushed out but not pegged

Watching every move and eager for the retrieve, but not going until sent.

despite the temptation to grab a pheasant that stubbornly refuses to run or fly even when the dog that is almost on top of it. For the dog working in the beating line life is always exciting and at times borders on the frantic. He is running about surrounded by the scent and sight of pheasants, hearing the sound of their wings as they clatter off through the trees and the shouts of the beaters. There are other dogs running about, handlers' whistles blowing and the sound of shots from the line of guns. Contrast this with his role when he takes on the mantle of the retriever.

Ideally, the perfect retrieving dog will sit patiently in front of his master's peg and watch every bird that comes over, mentally noting which are shot and where they fell. He will not, of course, make any attempt to take off and collect them until he is told to do so. Usually this will not be until the end of the drive, though in the case of a strong runner some guns prefer to set their dogs off on the scent straight away. A running pheasant can cover an awful lot of ground during the last twenty minutes of a drive and may never be picked if it is given too much law. Ideally – that word again – once the drive is over and the retrieving starts the gun will be able to direct the dog on to individual birds, picking the difficult ones first and leaving those that are lying dead in

The well-trained dog will stay where told until he is sent for the retrieve.

plain sight until last. All this requires a calm, patient, well-behaved dog that will not allow himself to be led into temptation no matter what the provocation.

Remember what we said about running pheasants and the need for the beaters' dog to resist the urge to follow up a foot scent? In direct contrast, following the foot scent of a wounded bird is exactly what we want our retriever to do, and to stick on that scent even if it takes him two or three fields away. And when he finds a wounded bird crouching under cover we want him to grab it, quickly, but gently, before it can start off running again. Is it any wonder that our dogs sometimes get confused when we use them in the beating line one moment and then expect them to act as retrievers the next?

Which Breed?

Choosing a gundog is not usually a decision based entirely on cold logic. We all have our particular fancies for one breed over another, for dogs rather than bitches, or vice versa, for a particular colour or type. We choose a Labrador and work it in the beating line even though we know that a spaniel would probably do a better job, or we buy a Cocker spaniel and expect it to sit by our side when we are shooting driven birds. Some guns will only consider owning a black Labrador: others insist on yellow or chocolate. Most of us would be hard put to say exactly why we prefer this dog or that one to all the others that are available, but there is little doubt that we will be happiest and enjoy our shooting that little bit more if we indulge those fancies and get the dog we want rather than the dog that common sense says we need.

If we look at the subject logically though there are some fairly obvious 'best buys' as far as shooting dogs are concerned. If you do all your shooting as a standing gun and never have to join the beating line then a specialist retriever is the dog for you, and the ubiquitous Labrador is undoubtedly the breed that will offer you the widest choice. The gun who spends all his time rough shooting and needs a dog to hunt out game for him and retrieve it after he has shot is likely to be best served by either a spaniel or one of the Hunt, Point and Retrieve breeds – though the latter will not be such a good option if the owner goes driven shooting as well as walking up pheasants.

If you spend the majority of your shooting days in the beating line then one of the spaniels breeds is likely to be your first choice. Things become a little more complicated if, like many guns, you do some rough shooting, some driven shooting and a bit of beating as well, possibly supplemented with the odd morning on the shore after ducks and geese. Do you want a dog that is primarily a hunter or a retriever? Is it better to get a Labrador and train it as a flushing dog or a spaniel and work it as a retriever? Of course, this assumes that you are only going to get one dog: another alternative is to get both a retriever and a spaniel and work whichever is appropriate.

Cold logic says get a Labrador if you want a retriever and a Springer or a Cocker if you want a flushing dog. Human nature says you will be happiest if you get the breed that you believe will please you most with its temperament, looks and style of working. It may not be the ideal breed for the job and it certainly won't be everybody's choice, but if it suits you then it is the right dog for you.

Buying a Dog

The one thing that must be stressed above all others when it comes to buying a gundog is that *it must come from working stock*. This is not because of any prejudice against people who show their dogs but because of the fact – and it *is* fact – that the majority of gundog breeds are sharply divided into show strains and working strains. The show dogs will look beautiful but in many cases their working instincts will have been bred out of them and they will be of little or no use in the shooting field. The exceptions to this are found among the Hunt, Point and Retrieve breeds where the majority of owners have tried to ensure that they breed for working ability as well as looks. Even so, if you are buying a puppy you must ensure that it comes from working parents: and the fact that the advert says 'Show, Work or Pet' is anything but a guarantee that your new pup will be capable of working.

Dogs are usually bought at one of three stages in their development: as puppies, as young dogs ready to start training, or as fully- or partly-trained adults. If you buy a puppy at eight weeks or so you will have all the fun of seeing it grow up and the satisfaction of training it yourself. You will also have to wait at least a year or two before your protégé is ready to start work and cope with the delights of house-training along the way. A fully trained adult will cost a lot of money but comes all ready to go shooting. You can see it working before you part with your money – and you will probably have to part with quite a lot of money if the dog is any good. A young adult ready to train may be a good compromise, provided you are clear why the dog is being sold after being run on to adulthood. Is it because there is some inherent fault, or just that the breeder has kept several from the litter until he decides which one to keep for himself? As always the lawyers have a term for it: caveat emptor or 'let the buyer beware'.

Training

There is a lot of fun and an enormous amount of satisfaction in rearing a puppy, training it yourself and eventually seeing it working. There is also a lot of hard work with no guarantee that the end product will be a success. Most of the basic training can be done in your back yard, but once you move on to more advanced lessons you will need access to open countryside and, eventually, to live pheasants, rabbits and the like. There is nothing inherently difficult about training a dog, though there is no doubt that some people are better suited to it than others. There are those people who have a natural talent for training dogs and seem to produce well-trained dogs almost effortlessly. Others find it almost impossible to train a dog, or even to handle a dog that has been trained properly by someone else.

Training for all gundogs starts with basic obedience lessons: sitting and staying, walking to heel and generally accepting that *you* give the orders and *he* (or she) obeys them. Lessons don't have to take very long: indeed, short lessons of ten minutes or so given every day are better than the odd marathon training session once a week or once a fortnight. Firm but gentle handling, good humour and consistency are the main requirements and the patience to ensure that each step in training is properly completed before rushing on to the more advanced (and more interesting) stages. Time spent on the basic disciplines of sitting, staying, walking to heel and coming when called is never time wasted.

Retrieving lessons can follow once the basic disciplines have been mastered. Again, the idea is to start slowly and simply with a single dummy collected from open ground where it is easily seen: blind retrieves and multiple retrieves from thick cover can follow quite a bit later. Remember that you are not so much teaching the dog to retrieve (which is something he probably does instinctively) but training him to do it *under your control*. The same applies to training the pup to hunt: his instincts will take him hunting but your training must ensure that he hunts where and when you want him to do it. There are dozens – probably hundreds – of books on dog training as well as evening classes and gundog training clinics run by experienced handlers so there is no shortage of advice and instruction available for the novice trainer.

An alternative to training your own puppy or buying a trained dog is to buy and rear a puppy and then hand him over to a professional trainer when he is ready to begin his education. This should be a less expensive route to a professionally trained dog than buying one in at the trained stage because you will have paid for the puppy, reared him and had him inoculated already. If you do decide to take this option it is as well to agree with your chosen trainer exactly what you should do in the way of basic training before handing the pupil over for proper schooling.

Training sessions can be organised all the year round, not just in the shooting season.

The most important days in a dog's education are those when you first take him shooting. Those early days in the shooting field are full of excitement and temptation for a young dog and it is essential that you stay firmly in control of him at this stage. If not you may never be properly in control again. The usual advice – and it is none the less valid for being repeated so often – is to leave the gun at home and concentrate solely on the dog for the first few times you take him out to experience the real thing. Remember: that old chestnut: 'The quickest way to ruin a gundog is to take him shooting': is absolutely true.

The Well Behaved Gundog

There are some shoots where you will be at a severe disadvantage if you don't have your own dog. There are other shoots where, unless you are really determined to work your own dog, you are probably better off leaving all the dog work to the professionals and simply concentrating on your shooting. And in between there are all the other shoots where ownership of a dog is a decision for the individual gun and you will be welcome with a dog at your side or without one.

There are very few, if any, pheasant shoots that could operate successfully without any dogs. You, as one of the guns, may decide not to bring a dog, but it is pretty much certain that some of the other participants will do so. On a heavily stocked pheasant shoot, provided you had enough manpower, you could easily run the beating line without any canine input, but without dogs to collect the shot birds it is absolutely certain that a proportion – possibly quite a large proportion – of the shot game would not be collected. If you are part of a small shoot that relies on hunting out wild pheasants in rough cover for its sport, then going shooting without dogs would mean that you would probably never even see half the pheasants on the shoot, never mind get a shot at them.

That said, not every shooting enthusiast has the time or the facilities to keep a gundog. This potential problem is counter-balanced by the many gundog owners who come along and work their dogs as beaters and pickers up even though they themselves are not taking part in the actual shooting. On a big driven day, with a full complement of beaters and pickers up, there is generally no need for the guns to have dogs, though lots of guns do bring their dogs anyway. Even on the small, walked up shoot, you can usually take part without a dog, provided that some of the other guns have their dogs along. So, in general, the decision to have, or not to have, a gundog is up to you, though some syndicates seeking new members will favour guns with good dogs over guns with no dogs. This raises the question of what constitutes a 'good dog'. Let us consider what sort of behaviour, from you and from your hound, will allow the canine half of the partnership to qualify for the 'good dog' title.

As far as his work is concerned it is quite easy to define a good dog. When hunting he should methodically search every bit of cover on his beat, miss nothing, ignore distractions like rabbits and hares (unless you are shooting rabbits and hares) and never stray too far from his handler. 'Too far' in the case of a spaniel on a walked up shoot might be twenty-five yards or so: a pointer on a grouse moor could still be well within bounds when three hundred yards away from the guns. Any birds found should be flushed (or pointed) and neither chased nor pegged. The good retriever will, naturally, be soft-mouthed, will not run in to shot or fall of game, won't whine or otherwise give tongue, will have great perseverance when hunting a strong runner, and face thick cover and cold water with equal alacrity.

It is a tribute to the standard of training and the inbuilt ability of our gundogs that many, many dogs, trained and handled by amateurs as well as professionals, do meet the specifications outlined above. In addition there are plenty of others who fall short of the ideal standards but are still good, useful dogs doing their bit to help fill the game bag on shoot days. And it must be said, there are also those dogs who are the absolute antithesis of the good dogs described previously: the hard mouthed, bone headed, pig stubborn brutes that we have all seen on shooting days but never actually owned ourselves. My dog is proudly independent: your dog is a little headstrong: his dog is totally out of control. My dog needs a few moments to settle: your dog needs strong handling: his dog needs a bullet.

Let us be honest: not all gundogs are paragons of virtue. Not all guns have the ability to handle a dog properly and keep him under control. However: if our dog is less than perfect there are things we can do to lessen the negative impact that he has on the shoot, other guns and other dogs. Just as there is the proper etiquette for guns to follow on a shoot day, so there are simple rules that will keep your dog from offending your host, the shoot captain, the keeper and your fellow guns. Mostly they are just common sense.

You have arrived at the meet. It may be on the front lawn of the castle or it may be a muddy farmyard. You park the vehicle and get out to greet the rest of the shoot members. What about your dog?

The first thing some guns do when they arrive at the shoot is to open up the car and let the dog out. He then mills around with the other dogs, piddles on someone's leg, starts a fight with a passing spaniel and then goes and relieves himself in a carefully chosen spot where everyone has a good chance of treading in it. Sound familiar? Take your dog out for a walk before you set off for the shoot so he can empty his bladder and his bowels somewhere that won't cause offence. And when you get to the meet, leave him in the vehicle until you are ready to move off for the first drive. If you've had a long journey to the meet, either stop just before you arrive and give him the chance to do what he needs to do, or, if stopping en route isn't practical, take him off out of the way of the other guns and dogs as soon as you arrive. Then put him back into the car. If he is well trained and reliable, and you want to demonstrate this publicly, you can always leave the tailgate open so he can sit and look out. There is absolutely nothing to be gained by having him mill about with the other dogs and get under everyones' feet, so don't let him.

Beating next. This won't be of any concern if you spend all your time shooting and don't have to double up as a beater, but there are a lot of small shoots where the guns' dogs do both. As we have already seen, there are shoots where only the best controlled and disciplined dogs are allowed in the beating line and then there are shoots where anything goes as long as your dog can get pheasants up into the air. You will know which category your shoot falls in to and, if you make the effort to be honest with yourself, you will also know which category encompasses your dog. If the shoot is category A plus, but your dog is category D minus, then there are only two places for him: back at home or on the end of a lead. If you set him off to hunt one wood and he ends up racketing through the next three drives as well, you will be less than popular with your fellow guns – particularly the ones who will be shooting on those drives.

Keeping a dog properly under control in the beating line is not the easiest of tasks. There is a great deal of temptation for him and, as we have already seen, the things that we don't want him to do when beating, such as getting on to the line of a running pheasant, may be exactly what we want him to do when he is wearing his retrieving hat. When it comes to sitting beside you in the line of guns though, there is no reason why he should not be well behaved. Sadly, an awful lot of 'non-slip' retrievers are anything but.

It is a fair bet that, in any line of eight standing guns, there will be one or two who have well-mannered, properly trained gundogs sitting beside their pegs, watching everything that is happening and waiting, patiently, until the drive is over and the moment comes for them to be sent to retrieve the shot birds. It is also a fair bet that there will be someone whose dog is racketing about and retrieving any pheasant it can find irrespective of who shot it. Even worse, it may be picking up one bird after another, spitting each one out as it sets off after the next and never actually retrieving anything. By the time the drive is over it has become almost impossible to know which of the shot birds have been collected and which are still to be picked. And some retrievers are, not unreasonably, reluctant to collect a bird that has already been mouthed by another dog.

If your dog is sufficiently well trained and well disciplined to sit quietly at your side throughout each drive and not be tempted to run in when a pheasant falls then by all means allow him to sit there. Not only does it look very impressive, but if you do decide to send him in hot pursuit of a strong runner, you can get him under way with just nod of the head, a click of the fingers or whatever command you use to send him for a retrieve. You won't have to start fumbling about to unclip his lead or unbuckle his collar: you won't be distracted just as the next pheasant comes over your peg. A really steady retriever is a wonderful thing and is exactly what all of us would like to own. But we must give a nod towards reality and accept that not every retriever is quite as rock-steady as we might like.

It is not that difficult to teach most young dogs to be perfectly steady during training sessions. It is when you take him out to work on a shoot day that the greatest temptation arises – just at the very moment when your attention is elsewhere. Instead of a raised hand, eye contact and a clear command to 'Stay' as the dummy is thrown, he is being largely ignored, because you are concentrating on your shooting. There are guns going off, beaters shouting, pheasants falling all around him, and probably one or two other, older dogs charging about and having a great time retrieving shot birds. Is it any wonder that he takes himself off to join in with them?

If you want to ensure that your steady young dog stays steady you should seriously consider leaving the gun at home and concentrating solely on your dog the first few times that you take him shooting. Going from the training ground to the shooting field is a big step for a young dog. If he feels that your attention is not on him then it is quite likely that he will slip off to do his own thing. And once you have lost control of your dog it is very, very difficult to establish it again.

But this assumes that you are starting with a young, newly trained dog. It may be that your dog is already experienced, and already adept at sliding off the moment your attention is elsewhere. There is nothing in any way difficult to ensuring that he doesn't go racketing all over the drive, stealing pheasants from other guns and generally letting you down in public. All you need to do is to put a lead round his neck and then tether him to the nearest immovable object.

There may be a convenient tree or fence post. Unless there is a very hard frost you can usually shove your stick down into the ground and tie him off to that – though if it is an expensive or particularly valued stick you may prefer not to risk a sudden lunge snapping it in half. You can buy rather vicious looking corkscrew devices that screw into the ground to make dog tethers. If your wife/husband/significant other is sufficiently malleable you may be able to persuade him/her to come along to the shoot and act as dog-holder. It doesn't matter how you do it, but if your dog can't be trusted to sit *and stay* throughout the drive, then for heaven's sake tie him down and spare the rest of us from his depredations.

If you travel between drives in some sort of shoot trailer then the rest of the team will appreciate it if you keep your dog and his muddy paws off the seats and off everybody's clothes, lunch bags and gun slips. If you are unfortunate enough to own one of those dogs that will insist on starting a fight whenever he meets another dog, then keep him well away from any opportunity to cause a ruckus. Use your own car to transport him and keep him on a lead and away from the other dogs between drives. You may not mind him having the odd scrap, but it is unlikely that the other guns – or dogs – will feel the same way.

Most shoots welcome reasonably well-behaved dogs. Indeed, the majority of shoots simply could not operate properly if there were no dogs to flush game and to retrieve it. However, the emphasis must be on 'well-behaved'. This doesn't mean that your dog has to be as responsive and tightly controlled as a field trial champion, but it does mean that you should ensure that he doesn't act in such a way as to spoil the day for others at the shoot. This may require a bit of fairly honest self-analysis because it is all too easy to turn a blind eye to our own dogs' faults. Just ask yourself if *you* would be happy if your neighbour's dog was stealing all *your* retrieves or jumping all over *your* brand new shooting coat with his muddy paws. Then apply the same standards to your own dog.

A dog is more than just a means of getting birds into the air and then into the game bag. Rearing, training and working gundogs can become a hobby, a passion and even a way of life. For many – perhaps most – guns, working their dogs is an integral part of their shooting life. There are few things in the shooting field more satisfying than the partnership between man and dog. Frustrating one moment and rewarding the next, for many of us a shooting day without a dog is a shooting day with half the fun taken away right from the start.

Well-trained chocolate and yellow Labradors waiting for the start of the drive.

7
TAKING PART

There are three things that have to happen in order for a pheasant shoot to take place. A pheasant has to be persuaded to fly, it has to be shot and it has to be collected after it has been shot. The absolute minimum staffing level for all this to happen is one man with a gun, though it will be a considerably more efficient operation if we make that one man with a gun and a dog. That way the dog can do all the hard work and leave the one man to concentrate on his shooting.

Another approach to pheasant shooting would employ fifteen to twenty beaters in the 'persuading to fly' role, half a dozen people with dogs on 'collection' duties and eight or ten men with guns to do the actual shooting. There might also be eight or ten loaders to enable the guns to maintain the maximum possible rate of fire, a team of gamekeepers to organise the beaters and the pickers-up, a shoot manager to organise the gamekeepers, someone to drive the game cart, someone else to drive the beaters' trailer, plus two or three people to prepare the shoot lunch. It is to be hoped that the fifty-man team would account for rather more pheasants than the solo hunter, though that is certainly no guarantee that they would gain any more enjoyment from their day. Pheasant shooting is a very broad church and the way in which you participate is entirely up to you and the openings available to you.

The three factors that will decide how and where you shoot your pheasants are the same three that detectives look for in a murder hunt – means, motive and opportunity. In other words, and a slightly different order… Motive – what sort of pheasant shooting would you like to do? Opportunity – is it available? And finally, means – can you afford it? Once you've decided the answer to question one and, hopefully, established that you can also say 'yes' to two and three, you will be in business – or rather you will be in the business of looking for some suitable shooting

Paradoxically, the simplest and cheapest form of pheasant shooting – rough shooting – may be the most difficult to find. All you need for the most basic rough shoot is permission to shoot over a piece of ground that has suitable cover for holding pheasants. The problem is, that finding ground with shooting rights available to lease may be next to impossible in your part of the country. On the other hand, if you want to shoot driven pheasants there are any number of estates, syndicates and sporting agencies that will gladly arrange a day or a season for you – in return for a suitable fee.

You can also take part as a beater or, if you have a suitable dog, as a picker-up. Many shoots are only too pleased to welcome a spare body in the beating line, and you

Walking up through rushy pastures on a rough shoot.

may even get paid for your enjoyment. Picking up is a rather more specialised job and requires not only a suitable dog, but that you more or less know what you are expected to be doing. Pickers-up tend to operate alone, often staying behind to collect shot game after the rest of the shooting party has gone on to the next drive. In contrast, beaters are generally working very much under the eye of the keeper who should ensure that they don't make any major errors. If you are a real novice and want to get a taste of the atmosphere on a pheasant shoot then a few days beating with your local estate or syndicate is an excellent way to gain some experience.

The most important thing for a complete novice joining the beating line is to listen – really listen – to what the keeper wants you to do and then try to do it. Remember that you are a member of a beating line and that, unless you are told otherwise, you should ensure that you stay in line with the rest of the beaters. The line should be evenly spaced across the covert, not bunched up in some places with wide gaps in others. The best authorities maintain that the only sound from the beating line should be the tapping of sticks. It may be that the shoot where you are beating expects the beaters to follow that advice, in which case, tap away and keep your mouth closed unless to talk quietly with a neighbour. In practice, beaters tend to be quite a vocal lot, and you may find that whistling, hand-clapping and various grunts and whoops are also employed to encourage the pheasants to fly, plus shouts of 'Over!' when one does take to the air. Provided you make no more noise than anyone else in the beating line you will probably be okay.

If you have ambitions to becoming a picker-up it is likely that you already have at least a reasonable knowledge of shooting customs and practices because you presumably have a trained retrieving dog ready for a little work experience. If you are new to the shoot then try and make absolutely sure that you know where you can send

There is always work for a beater with a good dog.

your dog in pursuit of runners and pricked birds. A novice beater is generally working alongside other, experienced beaters who can prevent him making any serious errors. If you are picking up on your own and send a young, excitable dog in hot pursuit of a runner that legs it into the next drive where several hundred pheasants are milling about nervously because they have been hearing the shots from across the way… Let's just say you are unlikely to be the most popular person in the team. Make sure you know what you are doing and if you are uncertain then leave well alone until you can check with someone who does know. In general, pickers-up get paid the same or even a little bit more than the beaters, though I have heard stories of estates that charge retriever owners for the privilege of collecting their shot game for them. I can't see it catching on in my part of Scotland.

Most people looking to join a pheasant shoot will see their role behind the gun rather than in the beating line. Unless you are fortunate enough to own a fair acreage of countryside already, or to be on very good terms with someone who does, the odds are that you will have to enter some form of commercial agreement in order to go shooting. There are several possibilities.

The Syndicate Shoot

Running a pheasant shoot can be an expensive business. While it must be very pleasant to own a couple of thousand acres of prime countryside and have the wherewithal to employ a gamekeeper, put down a few thousand pheasant poults and then invite your friends over to shoot them for you, it is a sad fact that very few of us are – or are ever likely to be – in that position. An alternative for the majority of would be pheasant shots is to form, or join, a syndicate and spread the cost among the guns.

Steep ground like this is good for showing high pheasants but makes the beaters work hard.

There are various forms of syndicate with some operating on a cooperative basis, others being purely commercial and various shades between. I have a gun in a small cooperative type syndicate and our organisation is typical of many throughout the country.

There are ten syndicate members. We lease the shooting rights on a mixed hill and low ground farm and release pheasants and partridges to supplement the snipe, woodcock, rabbits, hares, pigeons and ducks that live on or visit the farm during the season. We all lend a hand with the work, building pens, making feeders, and generally maintaining and improving the shoot and one member of the syndicate acts as part-time keeper and pays a lower subscription to compensate him for the extra work. We calculate our subscription by adding up all the costs – rent, poults, feed, equipment etc. – adding a bit on for contingencies and then dividing it between us. Everyone does as much work as they are able and, so far, the arrangement has proved satisfactory for all concerned, though I should stress that we all knew each other before forming the syndicate and had a pretty good idea that we could work together okay.

At the other end of the syndicate spectrum is the commercial syndicate run as a business where one person – usually the land owner or the shooting tenant – organises the shooting, pays all the costs and sells places in the syndicate with a view to making a profit over the season. This type of syndicate differs from other types of commercial shoot in that the same guns will shoot together all season rather than each shooting day being sold individually.

Syndicates also exist in various forms that are partly cooperative and partly commercial. It is not uncommon for one person to organise and run the syndicate on a non-profit making basis but to waive his own membership fees in return for these efforts. In some cases the organiser may make a small (or not so small) profit as well. This fact may or may not be known to the other members of the syndicate, though it is not too difficult to calculate the costs of running a syndicate once you know how much rent is being paid.

The price of joining a syndicate shoot varies enormously in line with the quality and quantity of sport on offer. Obviously the running costs of any shoot will go up roughly in line with the number of pheasants expected to figure in the bag, with an enormous leap in overall costs occurring as soon as it is deemed necessary to employ a full-time gamekeeper. In my part of Scotland it is possible to find a place in a small, working syndicate where as little as £200 per season will get you eight days driven pheasant shooting. The bags will be modest, you will probably have to be a beater instead of a gun on half the drives and get your hands dirty when a work party is arranged, but it would be difficult to find any shooting that offers better value for money.

If you want to shoot lots of pheasants and have others do all the work for you then the price of your membership will clearly have to be a lot higher. The price attached to a gun in a syndicate will vary according to what is on offer – a gun at a shoot that can show really high pheasants from ancient wooded valleys and provide gourmet luncheons in the great hall of a castle will demand higher fees than the shoot offering modest birds from forestry plantations with lunch taken from the bonnet of a Land Rover. As a very rough guide, an eight gun syndicate killing an average of two hundred and fifty pheasants on each of eight days shooting would probably cost each gun between eight and ten thousand pounds. You could certainly pay a lot more than this and you might find sport at this level for a bit less if you look around.

Whatever type of syndicate you intend to join there are a few basic questions that

On this small syndicate shoot the guns double up as beaters.

you should ask before you sign up. With the bigger, commercial syndicates these are relatively straightforward: primarily how many days shooting are being offered and what size bags are anticipated? There will be other, minor details to sort out such as whether lunches are included and what happens if a day is cancelled because of bad weather – is there insurance in place, would another day be arranged later or would it be just bad luck for the guns – but provided that the promised numbers of pheasants are shown on shooting days the organiser will have properly discharged his obligations. How he does it and what he does for the rest of the season is not really your concern.

Where problems can arise is with the less formal syndicates where the relationship between the organiser and the guns is not spelt out in detail. Typically a small syndicate will 'sell' membership on the basis of the numbers of birds to be released rather than the number expected to be shot. This is fine if all the guns are present, or given the opportunity to be present, on every shoot day. However: if the organiser decides to have the odd day for himself in addition to the official shooting days and perhaps invites a few friends along, it is understandable if the syndicate members feel aggrieved – if they find out. There have even been cases where the organiser sold the shooting to two different syndicates and neither was aware of the other. This amounts to fraud rather than simply sharp practice, though in court it might be argued that, unless it had been specifically agreed that only one syndicate would shoot over the land, the organiser was legally if not morally within his rights.

There are several other ways in which disputes or ill-feeling can occur in small syndicates, often because people have made different assumptions about what is or is not being provided. Anyone considering signing up for a small syndicate shoot should at least consider the following points and clarify them in advance. That way there should be no arguments later.

Team picture: guns and dogs after an early season day at a syndicate shoot.

How many guns are in the syndicate? This is important: if there are sixteen or eighteen guns who take turns shooting and beating you are effectively buying a half gun. This is a common arrangement, but not something you want to discover only on the first day of the season.

How many days shooting are planned?

Are these all driven days, or do they include some informal, walked up days at the beginning and end of the season?

Are the guns allocated guest days? This is another common arrangement where a syndicate may have eight members but places for nine guns with each member having one 'guest day' when he can invite a friend to shoot.

Are the guns allowed to send a substitute if they are unable to shoot, or wish to offer a days shooting to a friend?

Are there any ponds, lakes or rivers where duck can be flighted and are the syndicate members allowed to shoot them? If so, what arrangements will be made to share out this shooting between the members?

Are the syndicate members allowed access to the ground to shoot rabbits and pigeons other than on organised shoot days?

Are the syndicate members allowed to go rough shooting away from the main coverts? Many shoots have outlying bits of ground that are never shot on formal days but can offer good, informal sport for a couple of guns and their dogs. Are these areas open to the members? Strictly off limits? Going to be shot on walked up days?

What about work parties? Lots of syndicates organise work parties when they expect (hope) the guns will come along a build pens, cut rides, dig ponds, put out feeders or do some other of the many things that always need doing on a shoot. If your syndicate does this you should establish how many work parties are going to be organised and whether attendance is voluntary or compulsory. There is a great deal of difference between turning out once or twice a year to help with a specific task and finding that you are expected to spend every Sunday from August to January filling feeders.

This list may read as though becoming a member of a syndicate will mean endless arguments about who is entitled to do what, and when. In general that simply isn't the case, but complications do arise and ill-feeling can result simply from misunderstandings between members and the organiser. Beyond that, syndicates do exist where one or two members will blatantly take advantage of the rest of their fellow guns. If you are unfortunate enough to find yourself in such a situation the simplest thing is to look for another syndicate. There are plenty of good ones about.

Commercial Shoots

A 'commercial' shoot in this context refers to the type of enterprise that lets shooting by the day rather than by the season as is the case with syndicate shoots. In general commercial shoots tend to deal in larger numbers of pheasants, though some will arrange rough-shooting days for one or two guns as well as the formal, driven days that are their main source of income. Typically, days are sold by the numbers of pheasants expected to be shot and charged at so much per bird. This type of arrangement can

If you have any doubts about his steadiness keep your dog on a lead during the drives.

seem rather coldly calculated and totally alien to the concept of man the hunter going out to seek food for his table, but in order to be fair to both the shoot and the customer it is necessary for there to be a clear understanding of exactly what is being bought and sold.

Let us assume that you and seven friends have arranged a two hundred and fifty bird day at a shoot that can show spectacularly high pheasants. None of you are particularly good shots and by the end of the eighth drive you have expended well over a thousand cartridges for only a hundred pheasants in the bag. Has the shoot organiser fulfilled his obligations to you? Or consider another hypothetical situation where you have eight extremely competent shots and the pheasants are reasonable but eminently shootable. By lunchtime you have already killed two hundred and seventy birds. Do you go on and have another four drives after lunch? And if so, do you have to pay extra for the pheasants you shoot? These are questions that need to be answered before the shoot takes place.

In the first case, if you arrange to shoot high pheasants with a team of guns that are not really up to the task it is hardly the fault of the shoot organiser if you don't get your full bag – provided that he has sent enough birds over the guns for the bag to have been achieved with better marksmanship. The second case will depend on whether you contracted to shoot a particular number of birds, or have taken a day's pheasant shooting with eight drives and no limit on the bag. (This would be an unusual arrangement to say the least.) In practice a good keeper would try to present easier birds in the first case and harder ones in the latter. And it is a reasonable bet that the drives you would do after lunch in the latter case would not involve the best-stocked coverts on the shoot.

Normally though, when you arrange a day on a commercial shoot the contract will spell out what will happen if the bag is either missed or exceeded. If the shoot has presented you with a reasonable number of pheasants in relation to the proposed bag then they can probably be said to have fulfilled their obligations under the contract. Many – perhaps most – commercial shoots will have someone with a clicker counting the number of shots fired. It is then a matter of opinion as to how many shots per pheasant is a reasonable estimate, but if your guns have fired four or five times more cartridges than the agreed bag limit it is hardly reasonable to say that you haven't had a fair chance of shooting the bag. Assuming, of course, that your guns haven't wasted a couple of hundred shots at passing pigeons.

Where the bag is exceeded there is usually a simpler solution because the shooting contract is likely to specify what can happen under that circumstance. The normal procedure is for the guns have the choice of either stopping once the bag has been achieved, or continuing to shoot with an agreed supplementary cost for each extra pheasant shot. While this is fair to both the shoot organiser and to the guns as a whole it may be acutely embarrassing to individual guns who find themselves committed to paying considerably more than they had budgeted for a day shooting, or alternatively having to back out when the rest of the party has elected to continue shooting. One gun dropping out might not be a problem, but difficulties could arise if half the guns elected to finish and the rest preferred to go on.

Normally a well run commercial shoot with an experienced keeper in charge will assess the ability of the guns quite early in the day and then try and organise things so that they have, at the very least, a sporting chance of shooting the agreed number of pheasants, given the ability of the guns present on the day. There are exceptions: I know of one shoot that imposes a strict limit of three shots per bird – in other words, if a team of guns buys a two hundred bird day they will be stopped as soon as either two hundred birds have been shot or six hundred cartridges have been fired. Most syndicates would be more than happy to achieve a return of one pheasant for three shots, particularly if the birds were reasonably challenging. That said, the terms are made clear before a contract is signed, so it is entirely up to the guns whether they accept them or take their business elsewhere.

Driven pheasant days on commercial shoots tend towards quite large bags. I have heard the opinion expressed that anything less than a two hundred and fifty bird day is not worth the organiser's time, but there are sound business reasons for this. The costs of beaters and pickers-up will be practically the same whether one hundred or five hundred birds are shot. If the shoot manager is working on a margin of £2 per bird, then the one hundred bird day will yield a gross profit of £200. Pay a dozen beaters and pickers-up £20 per head and the whole of that day's profit and more has gone. Double the bag and there will be a little bit left over to appease the bank manager.

Most commercial shoot days are let to a team of guns who know each other and have probably shot together in the past, but it is also possible to take a day as an

Walking up with a Springer Spaniel on a steep hillside...

individual gun. This means that you will be shooting with a party of strangers: either making up the numbers where a team is a gun short or joining seven or eight other individuals. There is always a risk that you won't get on with your fellow guns, or that you may find yourself shooting with guns that are considerably more (or less) competent than you are. (Any of those things can also happen if you are shooting with a team of guns that you know already.) In the shooting field as elsewhere, some people enjoy meeting strangers: others are happier in company that they know well. If you fall into the latter category then taking an individual day with seven strangers is probably not a good idea.

The cost of commercial shooting varies considerably according to what is on offer and what the market will stand. Currently shoots are offering driven pheasant days at prices from £20 up to £40 per bird. You might expect that the top end of the scale would be offering the very best quality shooting in terms of high birds and spectacular scenery and this is often, but not invariably, the case. A high price is not a guarantee of high quality shooting any more than a low price necessarily equates with poorer quality birds. There are often bargains around towards the latter part of the season when shoots have a good stock of pheasants remaining and a few spare days to fill.

Commercial shoots are often run as part of another business such as a hotel or country estate and may offer accommodation and meals as part of the package. In some cases it may even be mandatory, with shooting only being let on condition that the shooting party stays in the hotel, while other shoots offer accommodation as an

...and a chance at a hen pheasant curling back over the gun.

optional extra. There are obvious benefits for the hotel with rooms being filled outside the usual tourist season and, for a team of guns who enjoy each others company, it can be a very congenial way to spend a couple of nights. Some packages even offer inducements for wives to come along as well.

Cancellation insurance is something that should be organised when booking a commercial shoot. Suppose the chosen day brings torrential rain, thick fog or a howling blizzard and has to be called off. Does the shoot organiser have to stand the whole loss or will your deposit be forfeited? In the first case you may find yourselves being dragged out to shoot whatever the weather: in the latter the shoot organiser may be more than happy to sit in the bar and watch the rain while his pheasants live to fly another day. If either the organiser or the guns have taken out shoot cancellation insurance these problems should be avoided. It is important to be clear which party is responsible for arranging the policy and to read the small print very carefully. Will the insurance still pay out if, for example, you call the shoot off after the first couple of drives, or are you only covered if the entire day is lost?

The Private Shoot

Back in Victorian and Edwardian times the great country houses all had their own shoots and the majority existed solely for the enjoyment of the landowner and his guests. Though the majority of shooting in Britain today is controlled either by syndicates or commercial shoots there are still some shoots in private ownership that are run without commercial consideration. At the very top of the list are those few remaining estates where the owners have kept the shoot, or part of the shoot, in hand and managed to resist the pressure to turn it into a commercial enterprise. There are other private shoots though, often quite small affairs, where someone takes on a shoot and runs it as they think fit, inviting guests to share it with them rather than selling shares in a syndicate.

Being invited to shoot at such venues will depend on who you know rather than on how much you are prepared to spend. For someone who owns a farm or has rented the shooting rights over some ground, running a private shoot can be an attractive alternative to setting up a syndicate. Obviously, they will have to bear the whole cost of the enterprise but this needn't necessarily require a lottery win. A small shoot run on a do-it-yourself basis can provide a lot of sport for very little outlay. At the opposite extreme the more well heeled may not object to taking on a keeper and putting down several thousand poults simply for their own amusement and that of their friends. The great advantage of running a private shoot is that you can run it your way with no worries about what will please the rest of the syndicate. There is also the likelihood that you will receive a fair number of return invitations and the satisfaction of a job well done.

Roving Syndicates

The 'roving syndicate' is something of a hybrid between the commercial shoot and the true syndicate shoot. It occurs when a team of guns form themselves into a syndicate with the idea of shooting together throughout the season, but source their shooting through commercial shoots rather than setting up a syndicate shoot on a particular piece of ground. This can be an attractive proposition in several ways.

The first advantage is that all the risks associated with running a syndicate are borne by the commercial shoot operators. Poaching, disease, predation, a shortage of bodies when working parties are required, possibly the hassle of employing a keeper and the financial repercussions if you are unable to fill the syndicate can all be forgotten. The other side of this particular coin is that commercial shoots are run to make a profit and you are going to have to pay for your shooting accordingly.

Then there is the chance to shoot at several different venues throughout the season. If you find a place particularly attractive you book can again: if the shooting is indifferent or the service poor you can take your custom elsewhere. You will lack the sense of belonging that comes with shooting over the same drives year after year and the involvement that some guns enjoy in planning and organising a shoot, but many guns would also see that as an advantage. You lose the possibility of the odd days rabbitting or pigeon shooting and having a handy place to train the dog, but these things are not always part of the deal with a normal syndicate.

Some roving syndicates have a floating membership of ten or a dozen guns so that not every gun has to attend every shoot. Although we are primarily concerned with pheasant shooting here a roving syndicate could operate right through the shooting season, taking in some grouse shooting in August and a couple of partridge days in September and October before getting down to the pheasants when the autumn gales have cleared the leaves from the trees. For a group of guns who get along well together the roving syndicate is an attractive proposition, though obviously not a cheap option.

Finding Shooting

The main source of advertising for shooting to let is the shooting press in general and the *Shooting Times* in particular always carries a number of offers of commercial shooting and places in syndicate shoots. Your local press may be a better source if you are looking to rent the shooting rights over some ground with a view to running a private shoot or setting up your own syndicate and of course, you can always place your own advertisement setting out your requirements. More and more shoots are setting up websites and if you have Internet access you can generally find out a lot more about commercial shoots than is available in a few lines at the back of a magazine – though the magazine can help by pointing you in the right direction.

The majority of syndicates never need to advertise for guns, finding their members by word of mouth and personal recommendation. It is relatively easy for someone with experience and local knowledge to find a place in a syndicate, but much harder for the novice or newcomer to an area. If you are a member of one of the field sports associations such as BASC (The British Association for Shooting and Conservation), the Countryside Alliance The National Gamekeepers Organisation or the Game Conservancy you may make some useful contacts if you attend their meetings.

Getting involved with local shoots as a beater or picker-up can also be useful in picking up tips about where shooting may be available. Some syndicates are naturally reluctant to offer a place to a complete stranger so time spent making friends with the guns, keepers and beaters on a local shoot may stand you in good stead when a vacancy occurs. Of course, this presupposes that your behaviour (and that of your dog if you have one) will lead to a recommendation rather than a warning off when the shoot captain makes his enquiries.

Which brings us to the matter of what is acceptable behaviour at a pheasant shoot?

Custom, Safety and Etiquette

Pheasant shooting has not been established for as long as some other fieldsports and is thus not quite so bound up with archaic language or traditional customs as fox hunting or falconry for example. There are though certain unwritten rules that will be observed, particularly on driven pheasant shoots, mostly concerned with sportsmanship, politeness and consideration towards the other people taking part in the shoot whether they are guns, beaters, keepers, pickers-up, land owners, agents or shoot managers.

The very first thing that every gun should ensure is that they arrive at the shoot in plenty of time. 'Draw for pegs and move off at 9:30' does not mean turn up on the stroke of 9:30 then hold everyone up for ten minutes while you put on your boots and waterproofs, fill your cartridge bag, assemble the gun and hunt through the car for the gloves you are almost sure are there somewhere. Even worse is to arrive late and expect everyone to be waiting for you. If all shoots held the draw and set off for the first drive exactly on time, irrespective of whether all the guns had arrived or not, there would be a lot less late arrivals who had been 'unavoidably delayed' on their way to the shoot.

When the guns are called over to draw for pegs go straight away: don't expect the rest of the team to wait while you finish your telling a story or filling your cartridge belt. Listen to what the keeper or shoot captain is saying and don't assume that it will be the usual chat that you've heard half a dozen times before. There may be something different this week and it may be important. If he says 'No ground game,' or 'Please shoot foxes if it can be done safely,' then make sure you remember and don't start bowling over rabbits or raising your cap with a polite 'Gone away,' if Reynard slips out of the wood in front of your peg. (If you happen to be a hunting man and consider shooting a fox akin to murder, then your best action is to make a point of studying the sky looking for the next pheasant until the fox is safely out of range. With any luck your neighbour will be a man of less scruples and save you from having to make an awkward explanation to an angry keeper.)

Make your way to your peg *quickly* and *quietly*. Particularly late in the season when the pheasants have learnt what happens on a shoot day, excessive noise from the guns may see half the birds in the drive legging it off to the next wood before the beaters have even started. And a sure way of annoying the keeper and the shoot captain is for you and one of the other guns to be standing nattering with your guns in their slips when the first pheasants start to fly over the line.

Leave your mobile phone at home or in the car. If you can't bear to be parted from it then at least switch the ring tone off so it doesn't annoy the rest of the guns. Don't even *think* about making a call, short of an absolutely dire emergency. And preferably not even

Dogs racing about during the pre-shoot briefing are a needless distraction.

then. If your business or your social life is so important that you can't leave it for six or seven hours then stay at home/work and let someone else shoot the pheasants.

Unless you have been specifically instructed to shoot them – at an end of season shoot with too many birds left on the ground perhaps – leave low pheasants alone. Hopefully they will fly better next time through. It doesn't matter that your neighbour may be blasting off at every bird that doesn't actually have its feet on the ground. The fact that he is no sportsman does not mean that you have to emulate him. Leave the low ones alone and hope that perhaps he will take a lead from you.

Don't shoot your neighbours' birds. That may seem too obvious to need stating but it is a fact that some guns will shoot at everything they think is in range even when it is heading directly towards the gun on the next peg. There may be times when birds are curling and swinging across the line when it is difficult to be sure who has 'ownership' of an oncoming pheasant. If you are not sure it is probably best to say 'Yours,' and leave it for your neighbour. He may well return the compliment before the drive is over. If, as sometimes can happen, a pheasant pretty much splits the difference between two pegs and is shot simultaneously by both guns the polite thing to do is to turn to your neighbour and say 'Yours I think.' You may well find him in the process of saying exactly the same thing to you.

If you have a dog keep him under control. If you can't keep him under control leave him at home. If you can't control him and can't bear to leave him behind, then keep him on a lead. Constantly having to whistle and shout at a wild dog isn't going to do anything to make your day more fun. It isn't going to make mine any better either.

Treat dead game with respect: here sorting grouse into old and young after a day on the hill.

Try to keep an accurate count of how many birds you have to pick and where they fell so that the pickers-up will know when all the birds have been collected. If you can say with certainty that there are six birds to pick on the banking behind you then whoever is picking up will probably keep hunting until all six are picked even if one or two are difficult to find. If you are vague about the numbers – 'a few', or 'several' – there is every chance that once the obvious ones are collected he or she will move on to the next drive. And as for the ones you missed: accept that you missed them and don't send someone half a mile across the valley to look for 'two or three that were definitely hard hit' when you know in your heart that they were nothing of the kind.

Don't waste time unnecessarily between drives. Note that what is 'unnecessary' on one shoot may be essential on another. If there are no pickers-up then you should ensure that, as far as is practicable, all your birds are collected before going on to the next drive. To shoot a pheasant and then just wander off and leave it is inexcusable. But! If there are pickers-up employed specifically to collect shot birds it is bad manners to hold everyone else up just so that you can show off your dog's ability on a runner.

Unless you are actually standing at your peg expecting a shot, or acting as a walking gun, always carry your gun open and empty or, preferably, put it in a gunslip.

Treat dead game with respect. Shot birds should never be slung in a heap in the back of a Land Rover, there to be trampled by boots and paws. It is not just a mark of respect: game that is properly handled will stay fresher and ultimately taste better than game that has been slung around, piled up in a heap and generally abused.

When your form deserts you and you shoot badly keep your explanations and excuses to yourself. Everyone shoots badly from time to time, and no one will think any the worse of you if you miss a stream of 'easy' pheasants. They may not even notice unless you draw their attention to it. If, by way of contrast, you are shooting exceptionally well, there is no need to boast. Your neighbours will almost certainly have seen and taken note.

When fences have to be climbed or ditches crossed it is much safer if you give your gun to someone else to hold while you negotiate the obstacle. If it is not in a slip you should open it and show that the chambers are empty before handing it to someone to hold for you. Be prepared to return the compliment once you are safely over and hold his gun for the next man across. Don't try to be too helpful and hold four or five guns at the same time unless they are safely ensconced in gun slips. Clinking barrels together, even quite gently, can cause dents that are expensive to repair.

Pheasant shooting is generally less dangerous to guns and beaters than grouse or partridge shooting where the birds tend to fly closer to the ground. With low flying game there is always a danger of swinging through the line or firing a shot in the direction of the beaters in front or the pickers-up waiting behind. Pheasants not only tend to fly much higher than their smaller cousins, but they are normally considered unsporting and left alone if they come through the line without sufficient altitude. That said, there is always the possibility of the odd partridge appearing in a pheasant drive, a woodcock flickering out of the covert, or that, on steep ground, the guns higher up the hill may be vulnerable to a careless shot even though the bird was well above you. If, as a general rule, you never shoot at a bird – pheasant or woodcock – unless you can see clear sky beneath it, you are unlikely to fire a dangerous shot. In particular,

It is much easier and safer to cross a fence if someone takes your gun for you.

beware of shooting at those pheasants that curl back along the edge of a wood. You may not be able to see them, but there will be beaters and stops working in among the trees. They will not be amused by the sound of an ounce of shot rattling through the branches around their ears.

When you are standing at your peg – indeed, at any time when you are holding a gun, loaded or otherwise – you should ensure that the muzzles are pointed in such a direction that, in the unlikely event of an accidental discharge, the shot would vent itself into the ground or up into the sky without causing harm to anyone. And that goes for dogs as well as humans. If your dog is sitting in front of you at your peg make sure that you are not holding a loaded gun over your forearm with the muzzles pointing directly at him.

Take an interest in everything that is going on around you. I once picked up at a shoot where the guns simply wandered off as soon as the drive was over with no attempt to collect the shot birds or even to let anyone know how many they had to pick. If all you are interested in is letting off your gun you would be better off shooting clay pigeons. A driven pheasant shoot is an exercise in teamwork with beaters, guns and pickers-up all having a part to play. Which brings us to our next point.

Be polite and friendly towards the beaters, keepers and pickers-up who are working hard to ensure that you enjoy your day's sport. A few words of thanks to the keeper when the pheasants have flown well, a bit of sympathy when the beaters emerge soaking wet from waist high kale, a compliment on a smart bit of dog work or just a

Always carry your gun with the muzzles pointing in a safe direction.

shared joke between drives goes a long way to fostering team spirit and letting everyone know that their hard work is appreciated.

Don't forget to thank your host and the keeper personally at the end of the day. Letter writing is becoming something of a lost art in these days of emails and text messaging, but there is no doubt that a nicely written thank-you letter dropping through the letterbox a day or two after the shoot shows that you not only enjoyed your day but have taken a little bit of time and trouble to say so.

If your shoot takes place somewhere that is open to the general public be polite to them even if they are wandering right across the drive dressed up in their Day-Glo cagoules. There are well organised campaigns to try and ban all fieldsports and the last thing we need is to add to its supporters by being rude to previously uncommitted voters. A few seconds spent explaining what is going on and perhaps politely requesting that they wait a few minutes before taking the footpath through the woods is far better than bawling obscenities at some innocent hiker. Just ask yourself which approach would be more effective if the positions were reversed?

If an old lady walking her pet dog or someone on a horse appears during a drive – even if they are not strictly supposed to be there – curb your enthusiasm and don't go blasting off at a pheasant just as they are passing you. In the case of the horse and rider this could be seriously dangerous. If you have some way of contacting the beaters it would make sense to pause the drive for a few minutes until they are safely out of the way.

At most shoots it is customary to give the keeper a tip at the end of the day. Keepering is not a well paid profession and many keepers rely heavily on their tips to bring their wages up to a reasonable level. If you are unsure about how big a tip to give then have a word with your fellow guns and see what they consider appropriate, but don't be afraid to give more (or less) if you feel so inclined. I always feel that a keeper who has been friendly and helpful has earned a bigger reward than one who has been surly, rude and uncooperative all day but you must make your own mind up.

All this may seem like an awful lot of dos and don'ts, but most of it is no more than common sense and good manners. If you are polite and punctual, handle your gun safely and act with respect to everyone and everything connected with the shoot you will not go far wrong.

Shooting

You can't learn to shoot from a book, though there have been many books published on the subject. If you read enough of them you may become an expert on the theory of shooting or you may just become confused. The written word can be useful in helping you with the way you shoot – the tactics you employ might be a better way to express it – but to actually learn to use a gun properly you need live instruction and practice. Once you've learned to mount and swing the gun properly reading up on the subject may be useful – provided the advice offered is sound. Anyone who has seen me shooting at pheasants will know that I am hardly the ideally qualified person to tell anyone else how to shoot, but I have made a few observations over the years that may be useful. Just don't ask me for a demonstration.

The one thing that is absolutely certain about pheasant shooting is that if you point your gun at a pheasant and pull the trigger you will not hit it – unless it happens to be standing still at the time. If a pheasant is flying – and what else would it be doing when you try to shoot it? – you have to shoot at where it is going to be when the shot reaches it: not at where it is right now. If you are mathematically inclined you can calculate exactly where shot column and pheasant will coincide. All you have to do is work out the speed, distance and direction of travel of the pheasant, then the velocity of the shot and the time it will take to travel from gun to pheasant making allowances for the spread of the shot and the stringing of the shot column, then factor in something for reaction time and you should be able to say with complete certainty that a pheasant 'x' feet above the ground travelling at 'y' miles per hour at an angle of 'z' degrees to the gun will require that the gun be aimed between 'a' and 'b' feet in front of it to ensure that the bird will be killed.

Precise though the method may sound there are two or three snags to overcome before the pheasant starts to fall. Where will you obtain accurate measurements of the height and speed of the pheasant? How will you ensure that when you pull the trigger the guns really is aimed 'between "a" and "b" feet' in front of it since the point of aim will be constantly changing as the pheasant flies (as will the required lead)? How will you compensate for slight but significant delay between your brain saying 'Fire' and your finger actually squeezing the trigger? And in any case, by the time you have worked all this out the pheasant will be safely pecking up wheat from a feeder half a mile away from you and your pocket calculator. Probably better just to swing the gun and hope.

We could apply the same twisted logic to any sport that requires the sportsman to make contact with a moving object, whether such contact is direct as in football or via an implement such as a bat or a racquet. The major difference with shooting is, of course, that the object to be struck is much farther away. Nevertheless, no footballer, cricketer or tennis player ever tries to work out mathematically the correct path along which to swing the foot, bat or racquet. They just get on and swing. We should note, however, that it takes practice to refine that swing to the point where the ball can be kicked or struck successfully. It also helps if the novice player gets some coaching into the correct way of kicking and swinging. Much the same goes for shooting.

The best way to learn to shoot is to take instruction from someone who knows what they are doing – and that means someone who knows how to instruct: not just anyone who can use a gun, however good a shot they may be. Knowing how to do something does not automatically qualify you to teach someone else how to do it. Make sure that your instructor really does know how to instruct.

The obvious place for any novice shot to gain experience is at a clay pigeon ground. It is a lot easier to learn to shoot at clay pigeons than to try to learn 'on the job' as it were by shooting pheasants. Clays have the advantage of being under the control of the instructor and can be thrown to order. Pheasants tend to be less cooperative. Half the 'secret' of shooting is no secret at all but lies in adopting the correct stance and mounting the gun properly. Get these basic items right and receive some good, clear tuition before bad habits have time to develop and you will be off to a much better start than if you come to your instructor for remedial work undertaken after you have learned how to miss consistently and taken time to hone your bad technique.

Gun mounted ready to take a snap shot when shooting in scrubby woodland.

But let us suppose that you already have some experience with a shotgun. You are standing at your peg, ready for the first drive to begin. It is a glorious day in mid-November, there is a clear blue sky, a sharp frost and although you can't see anybody you can hear the tapping of the beaters' sticks from the wood in front of you. There is a clatter of wings, the raucous call of a cock pheasant, and the first bird of the day climbs high above the beech trees and then settles into a gliding flight path that is going to bring him directly over your peg. It's your move.

Your best to chance to kill that pheasant cleanly is to shoot him out in front of your peg. An on-coming pheasant is flying into the shot string with his head and neck exposed and the pellets will strike with their own energy and that of the pheasant combined. If you wait until that pheasant has gone past you and shoot at it going away the speed of the pheasant inevitably reduces the striking energy of the shot. It is only a slight reduction, but if it were a high bird and near the limits of range it might be enough to make the difference between a clean kill and a wounded bird that flies on for some distance.

The way you mount and swing your gun at an on-coming pheasant is a more natural movement than the swing required for a going away bird. The gun comes up into your shoulder and then carries on in the same direction as the muzzles pull ahead of the pheasant in a single, easy, flowing movement. Once that pheasant has gone past the swing needed to lead the pheasant is downwards rather than upwards so the initial upward movement required to mount the gun has to be reversed. This obviously applies to the bird that is directly, or nearly directly over your head. If the pheasant is crossing out on your left or right side then the movement of the muzzles will be much the same irrespective of whether it is in front of or behind you. Even so, the points about the advantages of shooting the bird flying *into* the shot string still apply.

If you are walking up pheasants the majority of your shots are likely to be at going away birds. However, as they are also likely to be rising the track of the gun needed to get the muzzles moving ahead of the bird is again a single, flowing movement with no need to reverse the direction of swing. A climbing pheasant is also likely to be exposing his head to the gunner. I think this is the reason why walked up pheasants flying away from the gun are considered relatively easy to kill, whereas it has been my observation that very few guns are as consistent at killing pheasants behind their peg as they are at killing them in front.

As a general observation, the best shots that I have watched in action seem to mount and shoot their guns with very little delay between the moment the gun comes into the shoulder and the firing of the shot. Once a gun starts 'chasing' a bird through the air with the arc of the swing becoming longer and longer as they try to obtain the right amount of forward allowance it is a reasonable bet that the bird will fly on unscathed. If, having missed the first shot, the gun then fires a quick second barrel, swinging instinctively (and perhaps rather more aggressively, being angry with himself at missing the first shot) there is a good chance of seeing the bird fall.

The problem for anyone trying to shoot a moving object, pheasant, clay pigeon or anything else, is that at the moment the gun is fired it must be pointing, not at the object, but into empty space further along the object's flight path. Since it is impractical to calculate and impossible to actually measure off this distance, it follows that a successful flying shot has to be made by employing a combination of technique and experience. Technique is the way you mount and swing your gun: experience means recognising the sight picture that goes with a successful shot.

It is not difficult to calculate how much lead a pheasant, flying at a particular height and speed will require. Let us suppose we have a pheasant 100 feet up flying at 50 feet per second and that our shot charge has an average velocity of 1,000 feet per second. In the 1/10 of a second that the shot takes to travel 100 feet the pheasant will have flown five feet. Q.E.D., we need to aim five feet ahead of it and down it will come. This is a considerable over-simplification because it ignores the length of both the pheasant and the shot string but it will serve for the purposes of this illustration. Now let us consider how you can achieve that five-foot lead under field conditions.

In theory you could keep the gun stationary, aiming it a point in the sky and pulling the trigger when the pheasant was five feet short of reaching there. In practice this simply doesn't work. The only practical way to hit a moving object with a shotgun is to swing the gun so that it is also moving in relation to the target and fire when the correct amount of lead is reached. Which brings us to the first problem.

There is clearly no way in which we can actually measure off the required distance ahead of the pheasant, therefore we have to make an instant estimate even as we are swinging our gun. However: although the required lead will be the same no matter who is behind the gun, we all have a different perception as to what a five-foot lead actually looks like. Ask one person how much lead they gave a pheasant and you might get an answer along the lines of 'The length of a five bar gate'. (This is true: I've heard exactly that expression used a number of times.) Another man will tell you he didn't give any lead at all: just fired as the muzzles passed the pheasant's beak. Now we know that, if true, the second charge of shot would have passed five feet or so behind the pheasant, and if the average length of a five bar gate is around fifteen feet, then the first shot would have missed as well. So how come both killed their bird?

There are a several possible explanations. The most basic is that neither man was describing accurately what he was seeing at the moment he fired his gun. What we think we see is not always what we are actually seeing. There is also the difficulty that many people have in making an accurate estimation of distance. But beyond the obvious explanation of 'mistaken identity' there may be a difference in the way that each gun achieves the necessary lead when shooting at a pheasant.

Consider three of the most commonly described methods of shooting flying game. There is the 'sustained lead' approach where the gun tries to point the muzzles the correct distance in front of the pheasant and swing the gun so that they stay exactly that distance ahead until he has pulled the trigger. Then there is the 'smoke trail' technique which involves mounting the gun behind the bird and then tracking along an imaginary smoke trail until the muzzles catch up with and pass the bird, firing once they are the proper distance in front. Finally there is the 'mount and fire' method whereby the gun tracks the bird with his muzzles before mounting the gun, then brings the gun to his shoulder and fires in a single movement. There are other methods of course, but these three are probably enough to confuse us for the moment. Let us look at each in a little more detail.

The first thing to understand is that they will all work if applied properly. The second is that even though we may think we are using a particular technique we may be doing something slightly – even considerably – different in practice. In other words, someone who thinks he is shooting with the sustained lead method may actually be using the smoke trail technique *even though his perception of what he is doing says otherwise*. In the end all that matters is that we each find a method of shooting that works for us.

In the sustained lead method the muzzles of the gun are travelling at (relatively) the same speed as the target whereas the smoke trail technique requires that they are travelling faster. In the first case theory says that once the target has been acquired and the right lead established the shot could be fired at any time. If the muzzles are travelling faster than the bird though, there is only a limited window of opportunity in which to fire. In theory the former should be the easier method: in practice it is not since it requires you to make an accurate assessment of the required lead – and this requirement will change with every pheasant you try to shoot.

Using the smoke trail method means that you automatically make some of the necessary adjustments to your swing according to the speed, angle and distance of the pheasant. The mount and fire technique is similar in many ways though acquiring the right amount of lead is rather more instinctive and intuitive since the method allows much less time for consideration and making adjustments to your swing. Which – if any – of these ways of shooting will suit you is something that only experimentation and practice can establish. Some people shoot best when they are consciously applying a practised routine: others are at their best when they swing the gun

A good high pheasant flying along the line of guns.

instinctively. Only time and practice will establish what is right for you, and taking lessons from a good coach is probably the best way to learn and improve your technique.

One thing by which we nearly all handicap ourselves in the shooting field is a lack of practice. We arrive at the shoot, make our way to the first stand, take our gun out of its cover and load up ready for the first pheasant of the day. We may take a couple of practice swings, but generally that's it. The first time we fire the gun is when the first pheasant appears overhead.

Read any shooting book or magazine and you will find countless tales along the lines of: 'I missed the first dozen birds, but then I got my eye in and started hitting them'. It isn't surprising really. Can you imagine a tennis professional walking out onto the centre court and starting the match without ten minutes practice? A golfer hitting his first drive without a dozen practice swings or, in the case of the professionals, an hour on the practice ground? Those are professional sportsmen who train constantly, yet they wouldn't consider starting a match 'cold'. And yet we wander off to the first stand, load our gun for the first time in two weeks and expect to shoot properly straight away. Is it any wonder that we don't?

This probably doesn't matter too much if you are shooting on a day when a couple of hundred birds will be in the bag and you will have plenty of chances to get your eye in and your swing working properly. It isn't so good on the smaller shoot though where the total bag might be only fifty birds between eight guns. If you miss the first dozen shots you will probably have missed every bird that comes over you all day.

Having posed the question I must confess that I'm not sure what the answer might be. I suppose you could try and have a quick workout with some clay pigeons before every shoot but it is hardly practical, particularly on the short winter days when you are driving to the shoot long before dawn has broken. Besides: the idea of actually practicing before a shoot somehow doesn't seem quite sporting. If you are fortunate enough to shoot four or five days a week then practice is probably unnecessary: if you only get the gun out of the cabinet once a fortnight you would undoubtedly be a better shot if you had the time and the facilities to have regular practice sessions on sporting clays. If, like most of us, you lack both I suspect you will be quite happy muddling along, hitting a few and missing a few, having good days and bad days and simply enjoying your shooting. I think we all know that we *could* shoot better: perhaps it's as well for the pheasants that most of us don't.

Pheasant shooting is not a spectator sport. The only way to really experience a pheasant shoot is to take part: as a gun, a beater, a picker-up or a loader. If you are there in any capacity other than as a gun you may get paid for your endeavours, but the rates are rarely high enough to make the job rewarding per se. It may be the company, the chance to work the dog, a means of satisfying mans' basic hunting instinct or simply a way of spending a day out in the countryside with something to give it a sense of purpose, but thousands of people from all walks of life take part in pheasants shoots every day (except Sundays) from the beginning of October to the end of January. One man and a dog walking up the hedgerows or a cast of thousands (well, maybe fifty) at a big driven shoot: pheasant shooting is a sport that brings pleasure and employment to thousands of people.

8 RUNNING A SHOOT

If all you want to do is shoot pheasants or join the beating line or work your dog as a picker-up then you can limit your involvement with the shoot to turning up on shoot days and playing your chosen part. After the whistle sounds to signal the end of the last drive you can return home and get on with your life until the next shoot day. Once you have paid your fees or collected your wages (depending on your role) your responsibilities are discharged. Someone else has all the work and worries of the planning, organisation and execution of the shoot, so why should you or anyone else want to get involved? Why indeed?

Well: someone has to do it or there wouldn't be any shooting. And strangely, perversely even, some of us derive a great deal of pleasure from running shoots. We also come in for loads of frustration, anxiety and damned hard work, occasional abuse, considerable expense and sometimes the complete failure of all our plans to come to fruition but that only makes the good days even more rewarding – if there are any good days. So why would anyone in their right mind decide to get involved in running a pheasant shoot?

There is the obvious reason and the one that motivates most shoot organisers, which is that they enjoy shooting and want (or can be persuaded) to be more involved than simply turning up on shoot days. No shoot, other than the simplest of rough shoots, can be left to run itself and a driven pheasant shoot needs as much or more organising than most other forms of sporting shooting. There is always work to be done, both physical and administrative, from cutting rides and building pens, through filling feeders and controlling vermin to cooking the lunches and preparing the annual accounts. People get involved for all sorts of different reasons, some eagerly and others reluctantly, as anyone who has tried to organise a work party of volunteers will testify. What might they get back in return for their efforts?

Profit is the obvious motive driving commercial shoots where shooting is big business. It is also the reason that some people organise quite small syndicate shoots, charging the other guns enough so that their own shooting is subsidised to a greater or lesser extent. This may be no more than getting free shooting in return for their work, or it may involve quite a significant sum of money. It is up to the other syndicate members to decide whether the rewards are justified by the efforts – assuming that they are aware of the situation. Not all syndicates produce accounts for their members.

For full-time and part-time professional gamekeepers shooting is a source of employment. They are involved because it is their job, though there can be few, if any, keepers who don't have a keen interest in shooting and the countryside that goes beyond just finding a means of making a living. Keepering is not particularly well-paid – some would say that it is spectacularly badly paid considering the long hours, hard work and occasionally risky nature of the job – but there are invariably hordes of applicants for any keepering post.

Profit and paid employment are common reasons for running a shoot, but they are clearly not what motivates the thousands of enthusiasts who are involved with shoots run for the sake of shooting itself rather than as businesses. The work can be hard, there is no tangible reward and when things go wrong (or when someone thinks things have gone wrong, which is not necessarily the same thing) they get the blame. So why do it? Pick a reason from those listed below.

I like to get involved. Some people simply want to be at the heart of things. These are the people who get elected to committees, serve as parish councillors, organise the office Grand National sweepstake, the pub darts team, the school run rota and a hundred other things that I can't be bothered to list. You know who I mean: the pillars of the community/interfering busybodies without whom nothing would ever get done. Some people just have to be involved.

I could run things better than this. There are those people who always think they could do a better job than the present management, whether that management is organising a fifty bird day for half a dozen guns or selecting an England football team that could lift the next World Cup. In some cases they will be correct. If you criticise the current organisation loudly enough and often enough you will eventually either be co-opted onto the team or thrown out of the shoot. This strategy is unlikely to work with the England football team manager's post.

Someone has to do it/no one else will do it. Either a means of self-justification when the wife realises that every weekend for the next eight months is going to be tied up because you volunteered to feed the pheasants, or a sign that you cracked first when everyone was desperately trying to avoid the shoot captain's eye or think of a good reason why they couldn't possibly do it themselves 'though they would love to, of course...'

I'm the best person to do it. A touch of ego becoming apparent here. Some people genuinely believe that they are uniquely gifted with the ability to organise others – and we are not just talking about shooting here. Some people undoubtedly do have this ability, but it has been my experience that they are rarely the ones who brag most loudly about having it.

It's my ball so I make the rules. If you own the ground or hold the shooting lease then you are pretty much in pole position when it comes to deciding who does what – provided that the rest of the shoot agrees with you.

Leaving that frivolous look at shoot management aside, the reason that most people get involved in running a shoot is because shooting is their sport and they want to have a deeper involvement than simply turning up on shoot days and letting off their gun. Small shoots that don't employ professional keepering staff have to rely on part-timers and volunteers to get the work done and, despite my earlier remarks, much of the work involved in running a shoot is quite rewarding in itself. Working in the woods and fields, seeing pheasants grow from day old chicks to poults and then on to fully grown adults, making plans and seeing them come to fruition and just simply playing a part in the overall running of the shoot all help to make the actual shoot days more enjoyable because you have a stronger commitment to the success of the venture. And, after all, somebody has to do it.

Where to Shoot?

The first requirement for any shoot is to have some land to shoot over. How easy this will be to organise depends very much on where you are living. In southern and central England land is at a premium and finding 'spare' ground may be both difficult and expensive – perhaps very, very expensive. Go far enough west into Wales or north to parts of northern England and Scotland and the search becomes very much easier and the cost of land or shooting leases very much lower. Of course, you may already own or lease some suitable ground for pheasants in which case what was potentially the hardest part of running a pheasant shoot is already sorted.

But unless you already have the ground, or have a suitable spot in mind, you will need to start looking for a place to buy (if you are very rich) or somewhere with a shooting lease on offer (if you are not). The obvious places to look are the sporting magazines such as the *Field* and the *Shooting Times*, agricultural magazines like the *Farmer's Weekly* and the small ads in your local paper. Shooting leases on low ground tend to change hands at the end of the season in February so December and January are the most likely months to find something advertised if a shoot is already established on the land. If you are looking for virgin territory then you can place your own 'shooting rights wanted' advert at any time of the year.

Some estate agencies specialise in rural land management and it is always worth contacting them and enquiring whether they have shooting rights available in the area that you want. Make sure that you explain clearly what you are searching for, especially if it is something outside the usual run of shoot leases. There may be farms on their books that are not ideally suited to driven pheasant shooting but that might make a half decent little rough shoot with the right input. Forestry companies often let out the shooting over the land they control though in some cases, where thousands of acres of blanket softwoods cover the whole area, those shooting rights are worth very little. Your local veterinary practice, if they deal with farm animals, may be able to point you towards some free (in the sense of not currently used for shooting) ground, and it may be worth making enquires at any agricultural merchants in your area. The big water utilities often own large tracts of land and may let the shooting over them; the Ministry of Defence is another major landowner that sometimes makes shooting rights available and even your local council may be worth an approach, provided the creeping tide of political correctness hasn't already turned them against all form of country sport.

Word of mouth may be the best way of finding out about shooting rights that are available, or unused ground that might be turned into a pheasant shoot in your area. The greater your involvement with your local shoots, whether it is as a gun, a picker-up or a beater, the more chance you have of hearing about something becoming available before it is snapped up. It also helps considerably if someone is ready to vouch for your character, experience and safety record. Letting out the shooting rights on a farm or estate is a considerable risk for the landowner and involves a great deal of trust on his part. Wild dogs chasing stock, dangerous shots being fired, field gates left open, plastic cartridge cases scattered about for sheep and cattle to chew, vehicles cutting up the fields, hordes of pheasants pecking up the seed when the fields are drilled, people tramping through standing crops… Any or all of the above can happen if the wrong person is offered a shooting lease. It helps – a lot – if there is someone to give you a sound reference.

Let us leap ahead and assume that some ground has become available, the rent being demanded is within your budget and you are considering making an offer for the shooting rights. What should you look for when you are making your first inspection of the ground? How do you decide whether the land on offer is suitable for your purpose? It depends to some extent on whether you have a fixed idea of the type of shoot you want to run, or whether you are looking to find a piece of ground and then set up a shoot that will make the best of whatever potential the land may have.

If you are looking to set up a pheasant shoot that will offer eight days driven shooting with a potential bag of, let us say, two hundred birds per day, then you need a lease over ground that has the potential to carry at least four thousand pheasants, sufficient cover to hold that number of birds or a clause within the lease that allows you to create new coverts, and suitable places to build release pens for all those birds.

Getting involved with a local shoot is a good way to hear about shooting ground available in your area.

Running a shoot can be good fun provided you have the right people helping you.

You will be examining the ground with very specific aims in mind. If you just want somewhere to go shooting then you are more likely to take a walk around and assess the potential of the land with a view to seeing what sort of shoot you could set up. Is it suitable for a driven shoot or would it be better used for rough shooting? Are there woods where release pens could be sited or should you rely on wild birds for your sport? Is there a neighbouring shoot that will provide a ready supply of 'wild' birds? Are there any existing pens that are fit for use or capable of being repaired?

While you are considering the prospects for pheasants you should also be looking at what other potential the shoot offers. Are there ponds that you could use to attract duck for evening flights? Any wet, boggy areas that will hold snipe? Do pigeons come in to the woods to roost at night? Take a walk round and see what signs there are of rabbit warrens. Is there much wild game on the shoot already, or a residue of released birds from the previous shooting tenant? Keep a look out for signs of predators: crows, fox droppings, rat runs under the hedgerows, feral cats and the like. Trapping, baiting and lamping can take care of most of these problems, but both require time and effort on somebody's part. Will you have enough spare time to make that effort? Can you afford to employ a professional keeper to do the work for you? There is no point in spending a fortune on stocking a shoot just so the local foxes are well fed.

Try to assess what impact the way the land is farmed will have on your shoot plans. Pheasants love root crops such as turnips and sugar beet, while kale, cabbages, sprouts and the like offer cover and the possibility of organising drives provided they are still in place when shooting begins. Spilled grain in wheat and barley stubbles is great for stopping pheasants from wandering too far but modern farming methods often mean that fields are cultivated almost as soon as the combine and baler have moved off. In many ways 'bad' farming is good for the pheasant shoot: unkempt hedges, little patches of rough ground left to run wild, weeds allowed to flourish among the roots and cereals, muck hills left to rot instead of being spread fresh from the cattle sheds, boggy corners that are not drained and ponds and ditches that are left wild instead of being cleaned out every few years may look scruffy but it all helps to encourage and hold game.

Good access to the shoot is important and becomes more important as you increase the number of pheasants you release. It may be practical to lug the food for a hundred pheasants on your back but if you are putting down several thousand birds you will find feeding them extremely difficult unless you have some mechanised means of getting your food into the vicinity of your feed rides or hoppers. You may be able to drive across a firm, dry stubble to your release pen in August, but how will you get food and water to your birds once that stubble has been ploughed and planted? Even if your Land Rover is capable of getting there without becoming bogged will the farmer be happy to see you churning up his winter wheat on a daily basis?

Quad bikes are a great boon to the shoot with their ability to go almost anywhere and to do so with only the minimum damage to the land. They rarely get bogged down and if they do are relatively easy to drag out, but they are not cheap to buy and maintain. Many farms have their own quad these days and it may be possible to arrange to hire or borrow it occasionally depending on the attitude of the farmer and his relationship with the shoot.

The pheasant is an extremely adaptable bird and, as we have seen, can be persuaded to make his home in all kinds of habitat. While it is obviously important that your prospective shoot will hold pheasants, before signing your lease you should also consider how you are going to show those pheasants on shoot days. If you are planning to run a driven shoot you should try to identify your drives: where the beaters will flush the pheasants, where they will fly to and where the guns will stand in order to intercept them. The usual practice is to feed your pheasants away from the release pen and then drive them back towards it, but other strategies can be devised to suit local circumstances. If your plans tend more towards rough shooting and walking up pheasants with your dog then you will be looking to have your pheasants spread about over the shoot rather than concentrated in coverts. Will there be suitable holding cover for them at the end of the season, or will all the fields be bare plough by then?

If you are relatively new to running a shoot it is well worth enlisting the help of someone with experience to assess the potential of your shoot for you. The Game Conservancy have professional advisors who will do this for a price or you may know someone locally who will be willing to look around and give you the benefit of his opinion. Setting up a shoot from scratch inevitably involves a certain amount of 'try it and see what happens' since the pheasants will not be privy to your plans and may not cooperate fully when shooting begins.

Once you have made your mind up that the shoot is suitable for you and that the owner is willing to offer you the lease you should ensure that both parties know exactly what your plans are for the shoot. Shoot leases vary from multi-page documents

Root crops are attractive to pheasants and partridges but can be very wet to walk through on rainy days.

setting out in great detail everything that you may or may not do, to agreements that are nothing more than a handshake and a general understanding that you are now the shooting tenant. It is particularly with the latter type of agreement that problems can arise.

Suppose you have just agreed to pay the farmer £x per year for the shooting rights on his land. He thinks that you and a couple of pals will have a wander round a couple of times a month shooting pigeons and rabbits and the odd pheasant if one happens to wander in across the boundary. You plan to employ a full-time keeper, build six release pens, put down ten thousand pheasants and hold sixteen driven days for eight guns with all the attendant beaters and pickers-up along to help. You think you have acquired exclusive rights to all the shooting on the farm: he still expects to wander round with his gun whenever he feels the urge, and to invite a few friends along as well. You are assuming that all the work you put in during the first year will lay a firm foundation for the shooting over the next ten years: he is going to see how things go this season before he decides whether to let you have the shooting next year, rent it to someone else, keep it for himself or pack up shooting altogether. You will be delighted at the sight of thousands of pheasants strutting about the fields: he will be livid because of the damage they are doing to his newly sown crops.

Even a bracken-covered hill like this can be attractive to partridges and the occasional pheasant.

There is clearly a strong likelihood of conflict arising in all of those situations. It is absolutely essential that both parties are fully aware of what the other thinks has been agreed. If the lease is arranged by an estate agent the odds are that all the necessary conditions will be set out in writing, including the length of the lease and any restrictions on the number of birds you can release – minimum or maximum. If your arrangement is less formal make sure that your landlord is at least clear about your plans in general and is happy with them before finalising your agreement. It would be an awful shame to invest thousands of pounds in building release pens only to find your lease being terminated at the end of the first season because of a simple misunderstanding.

Syndicates and so on

But let us suppose that you have signed your lease or handed over the rent in cash and are ready to start organising your shoot. What sort of shoot are you going to run? If it is a simple rough shoot with yourself as the only gun then you pretty much know what you are doing already, but there are several other alternatives. Do you intend to meet all the expenses out of your own pocket and invite friends to shoot free of charge? Are

The shoot captain chatting to three of the guns between drives.

you going to pay for everything up front but then defray the expense by charging guns to come and shoot? Perhaps you will form a syndicate and share the cost between the members?

It is the third option – the syndicate – that needs most thought. If you plan to run the shoot just for your friends then you can do whatever you want provided you stay within the terms of your lease. In many ways the same can be said of the shoot run on a commercial basis. If what you are offering is sufficiently attractive to bring in paying guns, and what you actually provide meets your paying customers' expectations they will book again: if not you will receive a sharp lesson in commercial reality. If you plan to run a syndicate though it is as well to ensure that your prospective partners are operating on the same wavelength as you are else problems will occur.

There are several ways to approach the setting up of a syndicate shoot. One option is to make your own decision as to how many birds will be released and how many shoot days arranged and then offer that package to prospective members at a price that will just cover your costs or else show a small/modest/enormous profit and see how many takers you get. In this case you will be responsible for running the shoot, arranging for beaters, paying all the bills and ensuring that the guns enjoy the sort of shooting that they have paid you to provide. You 'own' the shoot; therefore you take full responsibility for running it and can pretty much make up your own rules. However: many syndicates are run on a more cooperative basis with all the guns being, at least nominally, partners in the management and decision making, and this type of set-up means ceding control to the rest of the syndicate members.

Just how democratic this type of syndicate will be depends on the personalities involved. Some people like to organise, others are content to let them and if you have the right balance your syndicate should run smoothly. If you have too many organisers, or too few, then problems can arise.

A syndicate needs someone to look after the administration: to order the poults and the feed, pay the rent, arrange shooting dates and make sure that all the guns know when they will be, collect subscriptions and keep accounts. Someone has to keeper the shoot: feed and water the pheasants, control foxes and crows, organise the beaters, build and maintain the pens and feeders and so on. Finally, someone has to organise shoot days: decide which drives are to be done, organise the draw for places, see that the guns are properly positioned and generally keep things moving along. Three distinct areas of responsibility: the Treasurer, the Keeper and the Shoot Captain or whatever other titles you like to give them. They may all be undertaken by the same person, or by two or three individuals depending on the time and talent available. What is important is that it is clearly understood and agreed as to who does what: not left to fortune and a general feeling that things will get done by somebody eventually because the chances are that they will not.

Although it is apparent that the shoot will not operate properly if insufficient effort is put into the three areas outlined above, problems will also arise if too many people start trying to run things. If your shoot days are punctuated by 'discussions' – arguments is perhaps a better word – about which drives to do, where to position the guns, whether to break for lunch or shoot right through to the last drive, what is the best way to beat the next wood and the like then the chances are that you have a case of too many chiefs, or would-be chiefs, and not enough Native Americans. It will not make for a happy and smooth-running shoot.

Ideally, whoever is in charge on shoot days will be quietly but firmly authorative. The plan for the day should be agreed in advance between shoot captain and keeper, outlined to the guns, beaters and pickers-up at the start of the day and then implemented: not chopped and changed because one gun would rather do drive B first instead of drive A, or another has to get away early and doesn't want to stop for lunch. That said, neither does the plan have to be absolutely cast in stone. Circumstances on the day might mean that things have to be amended or adapted to suit a change in the wind or the fact that a stray dog has pushed all the birds out of a particular covert. Making adaptations to suit conditions is fine, but switching things round because one gun shouts louder than the others will only serve to erode the authority of the people who should be in charge. Make your decisions and stick to them. If you start giving in to the whims of others without good reason things will only get worse.

Don't think that I am advocating a dictatorship as the ideal way to run a shoot – though I know of one or two syndicates where dictatorship would be a fair description of the management style – nor even that things should not be run by consensus among the syndicate members, but having decided who is in charge of what it is best to let them get on with the job. If you don't think they are up to it you can always speak your mind at the end of the season. Just don't be surprised if you find yourself elected in their place. At least then you'll have the chance to discover at first hand whether the task really is as easy as you thought.

Costs and Returns

Forecasting the overall costs for a shoot is a simple task. Forecasting the returns is rather more problematic. There are the costs that you have to pay every year for rent, pheasants, feed and labour, and there are the occasional costs such as materials for release pens, new feeders, vehicles, hiring a digger to make a new flight pond or fencing and planting new woodlands. The latter are what businessmen call capital projects and would normally be planned and priced individually whereas the general running costs make up the year on year expenditure of the shoot.

There are two ways to set a budget for a shoot. One is to decide how many pheasants you are going to release and then work out the cost, the other is to decide how much you are prepared to spend and then calculate how many pheasants that sum will buy and feed. The calculations are simple enough once you know how much rent you are going to pay, the cost of a pheasant poult, a bag of pellets and a sack of wheat and the salary you are going to pay your keeper. If you have a keeper. And if you propose paying him. The same goes for building pens and buying feeders: once you know the cost of a fence post, a roll of wire and a hopper you can work out your budget fairly accurately.

There are a few variables to take into account. Do you buy pheasant poults at seven or eight weeks old, ready to release or do you start off with day old chicks and rear them yourself? You can even go one or two stages further back and start with laying stock and an incubator to produce the day olds yourself. Alternatively, you can forget about chicks and poults and buy ex-layers from a game farm and release them instead.

Ex-layers, being adult birds at least one year old should be reasonably savvy as regards foxes and cats and possibly men with guns, having survived the previous season unscathed. Their health will vary according to the conditions in the laying pen and how well they were fed and looked after, though it is certain that the hens will have had a long laying season and may be debilitated as a result. You will get a lot more hens than cocks in your batch as they are penned at a ratio of six or eight hens to each cock. Some shoots buy ex-layers every year and have no problems with them, while others find them difficult to hold. They are less prone to the various ailments that poults can suffer so the likelihood of a disaster occurring because of an outbreak of disease is lessened. Whether they will still be on your ground when shooting starts is another matter.

Rearing your own birds should be a cheaper alternative to buying poults ready to release. I say 'should be' because the more stages in the production cycle you undertake the more chance there is of something going wrong. The game farmer aims to make a profit, as he is entitled to do, but he also assumes the risk until the birds are ready for release. You must also offset the potential savings against the amount of extra work required and the cost of the equipment needed for rearing chicks. If you have to buy in rearing sheds, heat lamps, feeders, drinkers and sections for runs you are unlikely to start making real savings for several seasons until the cost of the equipment has been recouped.

There is an alternative approach to pheasant shoot management whereby all the effort is concentrated on wild birds and by improving the habitat and controlling vermin the shoot aims to achieve a sustainable population of wild pheasants. While you will certainly save money on poults and pens, keeping the foxes, crows, stoats, weasels, mink and the like under control is a full time job without which you cannot hope to succeed. To produce sizeable bags of wild pheasants is possible, given the right conditions, but it is likely to be a more expensive project than simply building a pen and buying in a few thousand poults.

Wild pheasants tend to fly better than their reared cousins, but they also tend to fly exactly where they choose which may not necessarily be where you want them to go. If you are walking them up over your spaniel this is unlikely to be a problem, but if you have eight guns waiting in line to the east while all the birds head west you may start thinking that a release program has a lot to be said for it.

There are shoots that kill a lot of 'wild' birds every year simply by preparing feed rides around their boundaries. This is especially successful where the boundary marches with a big commercial shoot that releases large numbers of birds. While such behaviour is not illegal it is hardly ethical. Pheasants will stray and most shoots get some of their birds from their neighbours though usually this is a two way process. Deliberately trying to draw in birds from your neighbours while making no effort to produce any of your own is unsporting, tantamount to theft and definitely should not be encouraged.

Rearing your own pheasant chicks instead of buying poults may save you some money if all goes well.

Only experience can show you what level of return you can anticipate from the birds you release onto your shoot. As a very rough guide a forty per cent return – i.e. forty birds in the bag for every hundred poults released – is somewhere about the average, but local circumstances can make a great deal of difference to what can be achieved.

In general, the more birds you release the lower your percentage return is likely to be. I was a partner in a small shoot that released four hundred and sixty birds in its first season and shot one hundred and ninety three or forty-two percent of them. The next year we released two thousand pheasants, shot on twice as many days and only managed to shoot six hundred and ninety three or thirty-five per cent. One of my neighbours used to regularly shoot eight hundred birds per season from two thousand released. When he upped his release numbers to three thousand the bag only rose to just over nine hundred.

I'm not sure why this should be. One reason may be that the more birds that fly over a gun the less the proportion of them he will be able to shoot. If half a dozen birds come over you in the course of a drive there is a good chance that you will be able to fire two barrels at every one of them, assuming that they come singly. Now imagine a

Game crops are a quick and easy way to create cover for extra drives.

big drive where fifty or sixty birds fly over your peg in groups of three or four. If you shoot at half of them you will be doing well. You can only shoot at two pheasants out of each bunch, so if four come together two of them will get away without a shot being aimed at them. If you miss with your first shot the best you can do is kill one out of four. Some will come over while you are reloading and you are also likely to be a little more selective when it comes to deciding whether a pheasant is high enough to be a sporting shot if it is one of many rather than the only bird you have seen all day.

Putting down an extra few thousand poults may just mean that the pheasants come over in slightly bigger bunches so you are shooting at two out of six instead of two out of four. Also, where only a few hundred birds are released the expectations of the guns are much lower. Beating through a wood that only produces a dozen pheasants may be fine on a small shoot but where the guns are expecting (and paying) to shoot several hundred birds in a day such little drives are not appreciated.

The way the coverts on the shoot are laid out will also have an effect on the number of birds that will end up in the bag. If your drives consist of small woods with open fields around them it is less likely that your pheasants will slip out of the drive on foot than if several drives are linked together or are made up of sections of a single large

Any little splash of water may attract ducks if it is regularly fed.

forestry block. Towards the end of the season pheasants become remarkably adept at making their escape from the drives before the beaters and their dogs arrive to flush them. If they can slide along unseen from one belt of woodland to another they will do so, but they are usually less eager to run off over open ground and, with a little forward planning, can probably be blanked in to the drive.

The thickness of your ground cover will also have a bearing on the numbers of pheasants you shoot. Bare, draughty woods won't hold birds, but it is also possible for the undergrowth to be too dense, especially if it spreads over a wide area of the wood. Really thick brambles, dense stands of rhododendron and the like can mean that a fair proportion of the birds in the drive never leave the wood. Even a good sprinkling of dogs among the beaters may not be enough to ensure that every pheasant is found.

There are other factors that will influence the percentage return you get from your birds. The skill of the guns is one. It doesn't matter how good you are at putting pheasants over the guns if they don't have the ability to kill them. In a way this doesn't matter as long as they enjoy their day, but clearly a team of experts are going to kill a much higher proportion of the birds that come over them than a team of novices. The quality of the birds will also have a bearing on the numbers shot. If you can show really high pheasants your guns will not only find them difficult to kill but will probably still be delighted with their sport. Missing a stream of 'easy' birds when all the other guns are shooting well is humiliating, but when they appear as tiny dots against the clouds and everyone else is missing them too most guns are happy to say 'Too good for me' and move on to the next drive. If they manage to kill a couple they are happy for the rest of the day.

If you start your new shoot by setting a forty per cent return as your target you are unlikely to raise your guns' expectations too high. After the first season you will be in a position to make a more informed assessment.

Beaters

If you plan to run a driven pheasant shoot you will need beaters. How many will depend on the layout of your coverts and the numbers of pheasants you intend to release. I shoot over a hill farm just north of my home where one drive – a long, narrow strip of trees – can be handled easily by three beaters and a couple of dogs, while another – a wide, steeply sloping overgrown hillside – would make hard work for a dozen men with a dog apiece. Like most shoots, we have to do the best we can with whatever bodies, human and canine, happen to be available.

How effective your beaters will be depends on their experience and their willingness to work, particularly where the cover is thick and prickly. This applies to dogs as well as humans. If you are lucky you may have a ready supply of keen, knowledgeable beaters within range of your shoot: if not you may have to make do with whoever you can dredge up. It all depends on locality and on how well you treat them.

Some shoots are able to find beaters willing to work for nothing, or for nothing more than the promise of a days shooting at the end of the season. Others have to pay, provide transport to and from the shoot and throw in a free lunch into the bargain. The going rate for a beater today is somewhere between £15 and £25, so if you need ten beaters on each of eight shoot days you can easily be looking at a bill for £2000 over the course of the season. This may just be a drop in the ocean of your shoot budget if you are running a big commercial shoot, or it may be more than your entire budget for several seasons.

A lot of small syndicate shoots solve their beater problem by operating on a 'walk and stand' basis. This means having two teams of guns who take turns at shooting and beating on alternate drives. In effect, everyone is a half gun and this arrangement may not appeal to some, though there are lots of shooting men who welcome the chance to work their dogs as well as shooting driven pheasants on every shoot day. When it is cold and wet the chance to spend every other drive in the relative comfort and shelter of the woods can also take the edge off the discomfort of standing in the open exposed to the wind and the rain when it is your turn to shoot.

The other advantage of the walk and stand syndicate is that the costs are spread over double the number of members and, in theory at least, you have twice as many willing bodies available when it comes to organising work parties or looking for

Don't forget the cost of your beaters – unless you can find enough volunteers to work for free in return for a Keeper's Day shoot.

volunteers to fill the feed hoppers. The shoot captain's task of arranging the drives needs to be done with a great deal of tact and sensitivity to ensure that both teams get a fair share of the shooting over the course of the season, but it can be made to work and when it does it provides a cheap and interesting way of shooting, particularly for those guns who like to hunt with their dogs.

Another idea that some syndicates use is to make it the responsibility of each gun to bring someone along to act as a beater, or alternatively to pay the cost of a beater provided by the shoot. This takes the onus away from the keeper and puts it on the guns and can work well provided there is good communication between guns and shoot management. If a gun is planning to come to the shoot unaccompanied it is essential that the keeper or the shoot captain knows well in advance so that a substitute beater can be found. If all eight guns turn up beaterless on shoot day, all assuming that the other seven will have brought someone along the prospects of shooting many pheasants will look pretty bleak. Console yourself with the thought that it is unlikely to happen again.

It is worth remembering that most beaters attend because they enjoy shooting rather than for the prospect of a few pounds in their pockets. It is a good idea therefore to try and ensure that they get as much fun out of their work as is feasible. It is all too easy to put your beaters off. Guns who are rude or a keeper whose idea of man-management is to scream abuse at his beaters throughout the day; woods that are choked with thorns and brambles and have no rides cut through them; even the lack of a simple 'thank-you' at the end of the day can be enough to make a beater decide to take his services elsewhere. Leaving your beating team sitting out in the cold and wet while the guns enjoy a long lunch in a warm dining room is not good for morale either. A good beating team is the backbone of your shoot and it pays to look after them. If you don't there will be another shoot near at hand who will.

Work Parties

The work party is something that happens mainly on lower budget pheasant shoots where the keepering staff are part-time or volunteers. Guns paying a small fortune for their shooting are less likely to be receptive to a request for help cutting rides or building pens than someone who has to reach deep into their pockets in order to fund their sport and is happy to lend a hand in order to keep costs down. Work parties are a chance to meet up with the rest of the syndicate during the close season and by involving the guns in the behind the scenes work can help to increase their commitment to the success of the shoot. They can also help to make them realise just how much hard graft goes into ensuring that there will be some shooting when the season opens. It must also be said that the work party is not always a bringer of harmony and accord within the syndicate.

It is a universal truth that, in any group of people, there will be those who are willing to work and those who are willing to let them. If you manage to put together a syndicate where all the members turn out and pull their weight when a work party is organised you will be fortunate indeed. Nevertheless, the work party is a valuable asset in the shoot manager's armoury. It can also be a source of considerable friction.

There are always things that need doing around the shoot and some are well suited to the work party approach, i.e. getting a crowd of bodies on site and trying to blitz the job in a day or maybe two. Building a new pen, cutting rides through an overgrown wood, digging a new flight pond, fencing off strips for game crops and getting all the hoppers filled at the start of the season are the sort of things that come to mind. In the first year or two of setting up a new shoot you will probably find most, if not quite all, of the members willing and even eager to come along and do their bit. It is after a few years when the shoot has become established and the fun has gone out of jobs like driving posts or cutting brambles that attendance will fall away.

This wouldn't be a problem of itself, except that almost invariably it will be the same four or five people who turn up for every work party while the others never come along at all. After a while it is inevitable that the workers start wondering why they should do so much when others do so little. If they get sufficiently resentful there is the danger that they will stop coming too.

A work party in action building the gate for a new pen.

I have seen various ideas advanced to try and get around this problem, though none that struck me as particularly likely to succeed. Making attendance at work parties compulsory, or charging differential rates for 'worker' and 'non-worker' syndicate members are possible solutions but can be difficult to administer in practice. How do you deal with the member who simply won't turn up to your 'compulsory' work parties? Throw him out of the shoot? What if a syndicate member is genuinely ill and unable to attend? Does he get evicted as well, or charged the 'extra' rate for a non-working member even though he has always turned up and done his share in the past? There are no easy answers. The best solution I have seen has been to make attendance at work parties completely optional: those who wanted to help came along and worked; the rest didn't. This way there were no niggles about people who 'should have been there but didn't turn up' because nobody was being forced to work against their inclinations. The volunteers just got on with whatever work was required.

The well-organised work party will start with a clear idea of what needs to be done and will have ensured that those attending will bring along sufficient tools to do the job. There is little point having a dozen volunteer ride cutters with only two chainsaws between them. Try to keep your aspirations for the day within the capabilities of your volunteer work force – something that will depend very much on how they normally spend their time. Sitting behind a desk for eight hours a day is poor preparation for digging out a flight pond using spades and shovels. Give everyone plenty of notice. If you telephone on Friday evening looking for volunteers to work on the Saturday you must expect some or all of your crew to have prior commitments – especially those who would prefer not to work anyway.

Legal Considerations

Recent years have seen our society becoming increasingly litigious. Prompted by 'no win no fee' offers from lawyers and encouraged by the prospect of huge damages, people a resorting to the courts in ever increasing numbers and, at times, being awarded large sums of money. *Anyone* going shooting runs the risk of finding themselves on the receiving end of a law suit, and for the shoot organiser the danger is enhanced since he may be held responsible for the actions of everyone else connected with the shoot.

It isn't necessary to actually shoot somebody in order to be sued for damages. If the sound of shots causes panic among livestock or puts somebody's prize hens off the lay: if the sight of pheasants falling out of the sky spoils the enjoyment of somebody's picnic or the very idea of killing anything causes distress to their precious offspring then you may find yourself in court and being held vicariously liable as the organiser of the shoot. Insurance at least against third party risks is a must for every shoot. You should also consider the chance of having to pay damages if a gun or beater is injured falling off the trailer or slipping when crossing a stile or even, should the unthinkable happen, is accidentally shot. A comprehensive policy won't be cheap, but failure to hold one could bring about absolute financial ruin if you were held personally responsible for a serious incident.

Many shoots insist that all their guns are members of BASC or the National

Gamekeepers Organisation or one of the other shooting organisations that provide 'free' cover for their members as one of the rewards for signing up. Everyone who shoots, stalks, hunts or fishes should be a member of at least one of the organisations that campaign on our behalf, though unfortunately that is not the case in practice.

It is a legal requirement that anyone who shoots pheasants should hold a valid game licence. I have never yet been asked to prove that I hold a game licence before being allowed to shoot, but I suspect that a shoot organiser could charged with aiding and abetting if he allowed anyone who did not hold a game licence to shoot pheasants. The Game Licences Act 1860 specifically states that 'It is an offence for anyone to take, kill or pursue, *or assist in doing so*, (my italics) ...any game, woodcock, snipe, rabbit or deer, without an appropriate licence. Game licences are available over the counter from Crown post offices, cost next to nothing and should be renewed annually.

If you are running a shoot you are also vicariously liable for the actions of your employees. This means that, if your gamekeeper breaks the law by killing a protected species or using an illegal method of trapping and killing vermin you can also be

A quick bite and a bottle of beer snatched between drives is all these guns need for lunch.

prosecuted if it was done with your knowledge, consent or on your instructions. Many shoots now specifically state in their keepers' contracts of employment that they must not use any illegal means to control vermin, nor kill any protected species.

Everyone is liable for their own actions, but when you undertake to run a shoot you may discover that you are also liable for the actions of others. The extent to which you are held responsible for what other people do will depend to some extent on whether you have done everything that might reasonably be expected in order to ensure the safety of the public and of everyone directly and indirectly involved with the shoot.

It isn't just the obvious things like checking that any new gun is an experienced shot, giving a safety talk at the start of every shoot day, ensuring that your shoot transport meets all legal requirements, and that your keepers operate within the law. Failing to warn a gun that there is a stop positioned behind the hedge, or allowing a beater to bring along a dog that chases stock could mean that you get sued for damages even though you are not directly responsible.

Still Interested?

We started this chapter by wondering why anyone would want to run a shoot. After reading it you may well be wondering still. However, lots of people do run shoots and mostly through their own, personal choice, so it can't really be that bad can it? I suppose the answer to that question depends on the shoot you are running and the other people who are involved in the shoot with you. Having the right people around you can make running a shoot a real pleasure: surround yourself with the wrong ones and it can become a real pain. Nevertheless, I have been involved in running shoots in one way or another for much of the past twenty years and I have no plans to stop at this moment.

There is a certain satisfaction in seeing a job through from start to finish. When I have helped to build the release pen, feed and water the poults, dog them in when they wander, control the foxes and crows, fill the hoppers with wheat and scatter straw on the feed rides I can truly feel that I have earned my shot at that high, curling hen. If someone else has done all the work and all I have done is turn up and take my gun out of the cover then, although I will still enjoy my shooting, I don't have – can't have – quite the same feeling of ownership, of having played my part in the success of the day, of simply deserving some sport.

I will probably miss in either case, but that isn't the point.

⑨

GAMEKEEPING

The original function of the forerunners of the modern gamekeeper was to provide meat for their masters' tables. Later, when shooting became established as a sport for the gentry their job switched from actually hunting to preserving game in order that the master might hunt and kill it himself. Keepering has developed in many ways over the intervening centuries but the main task of the gamekeeper is still to produce game so that others may pursue it. The ways in which he does this have changed somewhat but the general objective remains the same and this goes as much for the part-timer who only has the odd hours at the weekend to dedicate to his keepering duties as for the professional keeper who is on duty practically every hour of every day.

The number of professional keepers in Britain has fallen dramatically over the past fifty years, compensated in part by a corresponding rise in the numbers of amateur keepers. For the smaller shoot, releasing a few hundred or perhaps a thousand poults, the cost of employing a full-time keeper is out of all proportion to the rest of the budget. The shoot rent plus the cost of buying and feeding a thousand poults might come to five or six thousand pounds: say an eight hundred pounds subscription for each of an eight member syndicate. If they shoot forty per cent of their pheasants the cost per bird in the bag would be about sixteen pounds. Let the syndicate employ a keeper, pay his wages, rent him a cottage, supply him with a vehicle and fuel, a tweed suit, cartridges and a dog allowance and they would be looking at an extra twenty thousand pounds a year on their budget. Now the cost of joining the shoot would be three thousand three hundred pounds per head and the cost of each bird in the bag would be sixty-six pounds.

Of course, with a full time keeper to look after them they could release a lot more birds and bring the cost back down to something reasonable, but those extra poults would have to be bought and fed. Release ten thousand poults and shoot four thousand and the cost per head would be back to something reasonable – under twenty pounds – but the cost of membership would be getting close to ten thousand pounds per gun. Now that may be a perfectly acceptable sum for some sportsmen but it is well beyond the reach of the majority of us. Which is why so many shoots are keepered by amateurs and part-timers.

A keeper's duties can be divided into five categories: habitat management, game production, predator control, security and shoot management. The way in which his time is split between the various categories will depend on the local situation and the way the shoot is organised. If the aim is to shoot predominantly wild birds then most of the effort will go into predator control and habitat management: if there are twenty thousand day old chicks to rear and release then there may not be time to do anything much beyond looking after them. Time and money are the two great restraints for amateur and professional keepers alike, though for the unpaid volunteer there is also the question of whether he has the inclination to carry out some of the less essential work.

We will look at each of the categories in turn and consider what can be done to make a success of your shoot. Note that there are not really clear divides between each: when you are out with the fox lamp in the evening you are also involved in the security aspect of the job. Building a release pen or establishing a game crop can be seen as habitat management or as an aspect of game production. In practice, strict categorisation is much less important than simply making sure the job gets done and done properly.

Habitat Management

The basis of habitat management lies in making your shoot a more welcoming place for pheasants. It may be that the shoot is already somewhere close to pheasant heaven in which case you will be free to concentrate on other aspects of your keepering duties. Equally, your shoot may be the sort of place that needs a great deal of work before any pheasant can be persuaded to linger within the boundaries. How much work you will be able to do will depend, as usual, on the time and money available, and also on the terms of your lease. Paying for the shooting rights does not mean that you have carte blanche to plant game crops, thin out woodland, dig flight ponds and cut rides. And in any case, most of the habitat 'management' on the shoot may occur as an incidental result of farming operations that may or may not be good for your pheasants.

In an ideal world (from the shoot manager's point of view) agricultural and forestry work would be planned and executed so as to be as pheasant friendly as possible. Stubbles would be left uncultivated through the autumn, herbicides and insecticides would not be sprayed on field headlands, weeds would be allowed to flourish in root crops, grass cutting for hay and silage would be delayed until nesting pheasants had hatched their broods and so on. If you are lucky enough to own, or at least to farm, the land where you shoot then you may indeed be able to adjust your farming methods to improve the prospects of the shoot. For most shoots sited on agricultural land though, the work of the farm has to come first and it is up to the keeper and the shoot manager to make the best they can of what is available.

This may not be a problem. If you have sufficient warm, dry woods with reasonable ground cover to hold your pheasants it shouldn't matter too much if all the stubbles are ploughed as soon as the combine leaves the field. Indeed, it may even be to your advantage. Acres of stubbles spreading out to the boundaries of the shoot can be an open invitation to your birds to wander, and they may not stop when they reach your march. A field of kale or turnips, planted for agricultural purposes (as opposed to being planned as a game crop), may provide you with an extra drive. Equally, it may draw a lot of your birds into a spot from which there is no sensible way to present them to the guns and thus be a nuisance rather than an asset.

But these things are largely beyond your control and you just have to live with them, blank in those turnips on shoot days and hope they will be sown in a better spot next year. Reactive management– making the best of situations as they arise – is a necessary part of running any shoot. Beyond that though, there are lots of things that can be done to make the shoot more attractive to pheasants and it is these aspects that we should be considering in this section.

Two things that a pheasant absolutely has to have are food and shelter. Food is easy to provide: feed hoppers and straw rides can be set up almost anywhere: but shelter can be a little more problematic. The aim should be to create conditions that will attract and hold your pheasants where you want them and then to increase the odds of them staying by providing food for them in those spots.

The ideal pheasant wood would have some open, sunny areas, some areas with good ground cover and other parts with a decent canopy for shelter from rain and snow. Unfortunately, all too often woods become cold and draughty as the canopy

Game crops can be used to provide food and shelter for pheasants.

closes over and kills off the undergrowth that provides warmth and shelter for pheasants. One answer, if you are allowed to do it, is to open up some areas by selective felling that will let the sunlight in to encourage growth at ground level. This is not something to be undertaken lightly since opening up parts of the wood can expose the rest of the trees to the risk of windblow and mean that the next autumn gale will flatten the whole lot.

Before going anywhere near a wood with a chainsaw it is essential to ensure that you have the permission of the landowner. Trees are a valuable crop and may not be chopped down at will. Be sure that all parties are totally in accord about what you are going to do. A vague request on your part to 'let a bit of light in' might suggest to your landlord that you wanted to brash back the lower branches of the trees on the edge of the wood. When he subsequently discovers that you have actually felled fifty or a hundred mature trees to create clearings he may be less than delighted. Ideally, go along to the wood with the owner or the forester so you can agree and mark the trees that are to be taken out.

If you are not allowed to make clearings you may still be able to improve the wood for pheasants by trimming back the lower branches and piling the brashings up to make temporary shelter for the birds. This will have the added benefit of making it

Open, airy woods like this can hold pheasants provided there is sufficient ground cover.

easier for your beaters to get through the trees, particularly in softwood plantations where lack of ground cover and an excess of low, prickly branches can make the wood unattractive to both pheasants and beaters respectively.

Softwoods are planted as a crop to be harvested and modern timber operations mean that what was a useful covert today can be reduced to something resembling a First World War battlefield tomorrow. However: as soon as the old trees have been logged and carted away new trees will be planted in their place and, more importantly, the bare earth will quickly sprout a dense undergrowth as brambles, shrubs and native species like birch spring up. Apart from the lack of roosting trees this is ideal cover for pheasants. Surprisingly, timber harvesting seems to have little impact on pheasants. I have seen pheasants sitting in trees even as the harvester was slicing through their trunks, so don't worry too much about your birds being scared off the shoot. Once they get used to the constant whine of the chain saws and the roar of the timber forwarders they will learn to ignore them.

A new wood, or a replanted one has a definite cycle of usefulness as pheasant cover. In the first few years the dense undergrowth will attract and hold birds and still be relatively easy for dogs and beaters to get through. As the cover gets thicker you will probably have to cut rides each season, particularly where brambles have taken root.

These young conifers will soon grow into a dense, dark plantation.

The trees seem to be slow to develop for the first few years then, having reached about shoulder height they suddenly take off and form a dense matt of branches that blocks out the light and will eventually kill off the undergrowth. For a year or two, unless you have time to clear rides, the wood becomes a tangled mess that defies dogs and beaters alike. Eventually lack of light clears the floor of the wood and you are back to the stage of having to make clearings to let some light in or pile up brashings to give the pheasants a bit of cover. And then they cut it down and you start over again.

Planting new woodlands is an expensive business and generally beyond the remit of a shooting lease. A quick, relatively cheap and easy way to create holding cover for pheasants is to plant game crops. These are things like kale, rape, fodder beet, canary grass, millet, sunflowers, wheat, oats, barley and mustard that can provide shelter and/or food for pheasants. Sometimes they are sown as single species crops, but often two or more plants are combined to provide a combination of food and shelter for the pheasants.

Game crops can be established away from existing coverts in order to provide extra drives or they can be planted alongside a bare-floored wood to provide cover to compensate for the lack of undergrowth. If they are being established on a stock farm they will need to be securely fenced or your cover will quickly end up inside a cow or a sheep. You will, of course, have to compensate the farmer for the loss of production caused by taking part of his field to plant game crop. The Game Conservancy do a lot of experimental work with different varieties and combinations of plants for game crops and can advise you as to the best mixtures for your requirements and your particular area.

Another habitat enhancement technique pioneered by the Game Conservancy is the use of conservation headlands, or the practice of not spraying the margins of fields and allowing weeds and insects to flourish there. This is particularly valuable if you have a 'wild' population of pheasants and partridges that will rely heavily on insect larvae to feed their chicks in the first few days after hatching. Leaving a narrow strip of land uncultivated on the edges of fields provides cover for all manner of wildlife as well as making corridors that encourage pheasants to travel around the shoot. This may or may not be a good thing: these corridors can help disperse your birds from the release pen to the coverts, but they can also lead to birds wandering away from the shoot altogether.

In general, anything that provides food, cover or amusement for your pheasants will help to keep them on the shoot, attract other pheasants to the shoot and serve to increase your bag. Little patches of rough ground, unkempt field margins and hedgerows, straw rides for scratching, piles of brashings for cover and tin shelters for dust bathing can all be useful if you have the time available to arrange them.

Game Production

In theory the simplest way to produce pheasants is to let the pheasants get on with it themselves. Leave them alone to mate, nest, hatch and rear their chicks and then you come along when the season opens and take your share of a natural, wild resource. That's the theory. In practice, unless you put an awful lot of effort into controlling predators and providing the right sort of habitat for your pheasants to thrive you are unlikely to produce a large enough, sustainable shootable surplus of pheasants year after year to satisfy anyone but the most casual of rough shooters.

A lot depends on your definition of what is a 'large enough' surplus. If you are running a small rough shoot you may well find enough wild birds breeding to provide you with sport throughout the season, but if you are in charge of a syndicate that hopes to shoot several hundred (or several thousand) pheasants you are almost bound to run some sort of rear and release programme. How you set about this will, as ever, depend on the time, money and other resources you have available.

The production cycle involved in producing pheasant poults is simple. At the end of the season the parent stock are caught up and removed to laying pens. The eggs are collected and hatched out in incubators. The day old chicks are raised in a rearing unit until they are about seven weeks old and then moved on to their release pens. You can start off at any point in the cycle from doing the whole job yourself to simply taking delivery of seven-week-old poults. The earlier in the cycle you start the lower your costs should be (and note that I say 'should be', not 'will be') but also the greater will be the risks you take and the amount of work required. Let us start at the end of the cycle and work backwards, starting at the minimum amount of work needed and ending with the maximum.

Poults in the rearing pen being hardened off prior to release.

The easy way of releasing pheasant poults is to buy them from a game farm ready to release. If you have a good, reliable supplier you will receive exactly the number of poults you have ordered and you have every right to expect those poults to be fit and healthy at the time they are delivered. Most shoots get their poults between mid-July and the end of August so, apart from getting the release pens ready to receive them, the time between the end of the shooting season and the arrival of the poults is free for whatever else you want to do around the shoot or away from it.

You will, of course, have to pay the market price for those poults, including whatever profit margin the game farm has added to their total costs. In theory it is possible to save a substantial proportion of that cost by starting off with day old chicks and rearing them yourself. This way you save the profit margin and the cost of the labour involved in rearing. In practice, if you are unfortunate enough to get an outbreak of disease among your chicks, or a heater fails during the night, or a fox gets into the rearing pen, you run the risk of ending up short of poults and having to buy in extra birds to replace them: a situation that could mean that your costs are eventually higher than if you had simply bought all your poults ready to release in the first place.

Pheasant chicks need a brooder hut, feeders and drinkers, plus a source of heat for their first few weeks, then a larger run to allow them access to the open air so that they can gradually get hardened off ready for being switched to the release pens. They need regular feeding and watering and will almost certainly have to be fitted with bits to stop them feather pecking. They may need dosing with antibiotics if they get sick, the heater will need close attention to ensure that it is reliable and running at the right temperature, feed trays and drinkers should be scrubbed twice a day and any dead chicks removed from the floor of the hut. The cleaner and tidier your set up and the closer the attention you pay to your charges the better the results are likely to be. But it is quite a lot of work.

If you have access to an incubator then you can go another one or two steps back along the production cycle and either buy in eggs to hatch or catch up pheasants at the end of the shooting season and collect your own eggs. This is really an option for either the very small or very large shoot. If you only want to release a hundred or so pheasants then a dozen birds in a laying pen, a tiny incubator and a simple brooder unit will suffice and you should be able to produce those birds very cheaply. If you are at the other end of the scale and releasing twenty, or forty, or sixty thousand birds on a commercial shoot it is possible to make very considerable cost savings by keeping the whole production cycle in-house, though the initial investment in equipment and rearing sheds will be considerable. For the majority of shoots though, the most efficient use of your resources is probably to let the professionals do the rearing and concentrate your efforts on the poults.

A good release pen is half the battle when it comes to turning poults into well-grown adult pheasants. Give them as much room as you can to avoid the ground becoming bare and foul and try to ensure that your pen has a mixture of cover for shelter from the rain and from winged predators, open spaces so the birds can sun themselves and trees suitable for roosting. Make sure they have food and clean water available at all times. If the ground is a bit bare in the pen scatter a few bales of straw to give the birds something to keep their interest as they scratch and peck among the stalks instead of wandering off.

A release pen serves two purposes: it keeps the poults in and it should keep predators out. Check the netting regularly for any signs that foxes or badgers have tried to burrow underneath. An electric fence run round the pen a few inches above the ground is an excellent deterrent for foxes and badgers as well as feral cats and stray dogs. A good belt on the nose from a fence is often sufficient to persuade them to seek their dinner elsewhere and to give the release pen a wide berth thereafter. Various other devices such as fluorescent tubes wired to the electric fence so that they flash at night, a radio playing, or old CDs hung from the trees to reflect the sunlight may help to deter predators and a few tunnel traps strategically sited can deter stoats and weasels permanently.

My experience with pheasant poults is that they are most prone to go over the wire and start wandering for the first three or four nights after they are released. Always make a point of being around the pen towards dusk on those first few days and quietly walk your poults back in through the pop holes. It helps a lot if you can persuade a companion to come with you otherwise you may find yourself doing endless laps of the pen with a bunch of birds running ahead of you and stubbornly refusing to use the pop holes. Two people can bunch the poults up by the pop holes and hold them there while they filter gradually through into the pen. Once they get settled they will probably be quite content with their new home for the next few weeks, and then the urge to wander will strike again, though by this time you should have your feed rides

Some sort of transport is almost essential if your release pens are far from roads or tracks.

all set up and will be quite happy for them to explore – provided they don't explore too far. Then all you have to do is keep feeding them, dog them in around the boundaries if they seem to be wandering off the shoot, and wait for the start of the season. Sounds simple, doesn't it?

In fact, in a good year when the weather is on your side, the poults stay healthy and the foxes mind their own business, releasing poults successfully is not that difficult. It is the bad years, when constant rain turns the pen into a swamp, the poults insist on breaking out and the fox breaks in, disease decimates your numbers and the price of wheat doubles unexpectedly that you will wonder why you ever got into this keepering business in the first place. You will not be alone in wondering, but the chances are you will be back doing it all again next year.

Predator Control

There was a time when, for some gamekeepers, predator control meant killing everything that was, or might just conceivably be considered to be, a threat to their pheasants. Foxes, badgers, stoats, weasels, hedgehogs, martens, squirrels, polecats, domestic cats and dogs, crows, magpies, jackdaws, rooks, owls, jays and all species of hawks, falcons and buzzards were trapped, snared, poisoned or shot and the corpses displayed on a gibbet to show how well the keeper was doing his job. Many employers paid vermin money – a bounty for every predator killed – and this could make up a significant part of a keeper's income.

Nowadays both the predators that may be controlled and the means by which that control can take place are severely curtailed by laws that, at times, seem to be enforced with extraordinary rigour. If a keeper shoots a badger that has been breaking into his release pen and killing pheasant poults he stands a very real chance of serving a prison sentence for his action, yet the government can authorise the slaughter of twenty thousand badgers as an experiment to try to assess whether they spread TB to cattle. Indeed, it is characteristic of modern governments that they consider themselves above the laws that they impose on their citizens. The same government that buried millions of sheep and cattle in stinking pits during the foot and mouth epidemic of 2001 have since made it a criminal offence for a farmer to bury so much as a single lamb because, they claim, it poses a risk to public health.

Nevertheless, whether you agree with the law or not it is never wise to flout it. The publicity that ensues whenever a buzzard or a kite is found poisoned does great harm to everyone involved with field sports and may eventually contribute to shooting and hunting being banned altogether. Always act within the law where predator control is concerned. It is not just your own liberty at risk but the whole sport of shooting.

So what can you do to control the predators on your shoot? And what do you actually need to do? The latter is an important consideration. Predator control can be seen in two lights: as a vital part of keepering without which no shoot can be successful, or as an interesting sideline for the keeper that makes very little difference to the number of pheasants that are shot. Which view is correct?

If you are running a shoot that relies on wild pheasants breeding naturally, then there is no doubt that your only chance of success lies with eliminating as far as

Electric fence and fluorescent tube are part of the anti-predator precautions at this release pen.

possible the foxes and crows that will take sitting hens and their eggs and chicks. A hen pheasant is never more vulnerable than when she is sitting on her eggs, and her chicks are helpless bundles of nourishing protein for the first three or four weeks of their existence. A wild pheasant shoot can only succeed if the right conditions exist and one of the most important conditions is a near absence of predation.

But most shoots regard pheasants that breed on the shoot as no more than a useful bonus to supplement the released birds. Many of the predators that will take a severe toll of eggs and young chicks present no threat to poults at seven or eight weeks of age. The fox is an ever-present danger of course, but a well-made release pen protected by an electric fence should deter most foxes from the area where they present the maximum threat to your poults. It is also true that you will never clear your shoot of foxes, since as fast as you kill them others will come along to take their place. So is there any real point in predator control?

To answer that question properly means looking beyond the simple question of whether killing predators will result in more pheasants being available for the guns on shoot days. No predator limits its diet solely to pheasants, their eggs and chicks. Over the past half century there has been a steady decline in the population of all kinds of farm and woodland birds. It is likely that much of that decline is due to changes in farming practices, loss of habitat and the use of pesticides and herbicides, but the dwindling populations are certainly not helped in their fight for survival by an excess of predators. When a keeper traps or shoots a crow or a fox he is not only aiding the survival chances of his pheasants, but he is also doing a little bit to help all the other prey species, and for that reason alone predator control is well worth while.

There are other benefits of course. You may not have many wild pheasants about your shoot, but keeping down the numbers of crows and foxes will ensure that what there are will have the best possible chance of rearing chicks and adding a few extra birds to your season's total. Getting out and about on the shoot, lamping or checking traps and snares helps you to see what is going on and acts as a deterrent to human predators. And for many keepers, trapping and shooting foxes and crows is as much a sport as a job. So, while vermin control may not be absolutely essential in terms of the ultimate success or failure of the shoot – you could, after all, order an extra ten per cent poults just to feed the foxes – it is an extremely useful and often rewarding part of a keeper's work.

It is important to note that, when I suggest that vermin control may not be vital to the success of a shoot, I am writing only about pheasant shoots where the bulk of the bag is obtained from released birds. If you are keepering a grouse moor for example then rigourous vermin control is probably the most important part of your work, and the same goes for any shoot where the quarry is a wild bird that breeds on the shoot, be it pheasant, partridge, grouse, blackgame, mallard or even snipe.

The fox is the major threat to the pheasants on most shoots and is likely to cause the most damage if it gains access to the pen, particularly when the poults are first released and at their most vulnerable. In such circumstances a fox may go on a killing spree, slaughtering far more poults than it could possibly eat. This behaviour may be triggered by excitement at seeing crowds of frightened poults running and flapping in blind panic. There is also a very real danger that a fox getting into the pen may send hundreds of poults flying over the wire and out into the night to die of cold and starvation. Since you cannot mount guard over your pens for twenty-four hours a day, the most important step in fox control is to ensure that, as far as is possible, a fox cannot get into the release pen in the first place.

Good, strong netting, well pegged down and gates that are closely fitted and securely closed are essential, and if you are in an area where the general public may visit your pen it is as well to keep a stout padlock on the gate. A gate opened and left, whether through ignorance or malice, can ruin your prospects for the season in just a few minutes if a fox or a stray dog gets into the pen or if your poults simply stroll out and wander away.

Once you are satisfied that your pen is a fox-proof as possible you should supplement your defences with an electric fence running all round the perimeter and make sure that the battery is charged and the fence is working. Good netting may keep a fox out of the pen but it won't stop him panicking the poults and snapping up any that are outside the wire. A sharp sting on the nose from an electric fence has a good chance of sending him packing and the memory of the shock may well keep him right away from the pen in future.

Electric fences are also useful in deterring stray dogs and cats, though they don't seem to have as much effect on any badgers that take it into their heads to burrow under your netting. Unfortunately they are no help at all in keeping away any winged predators that may take a fancy to your newly released poults.

Poults are most at risk from the likes of owls, sparrow hawks, buzzards and goshawks in the first few weeks after they are released. Several hundred young

Poults are vulnerable to all kinds of predators when they first leave the pen.

pheasants clustered together in a pen represent a unique opportunity for the local raptor population. Plenty of cover in the pen, whether natural or created from piles of brashings, will help your poults to conceal themselves from hunting owls and hawks. Trapping, shooting or poisoning any predators of the hooked beak variety is strictly forbidden and could well result in a prison sentence for anyone caught doing it. Your best defence is to try and find ways to deter them from hunting around your pen. Various ideas have been mentioned already: hanging old compact discs from the trees to spin and reflect the light, leaving a radio playing in the pen, setting up scarecrows or attaching old fluorescent tubes to the electric fence so that they flash with each pulse. Any of these things may help, though it is likely that the predators will get used to them fairly quickly and learn to ignore them. Provided they work during the first few weeks after release they will have done their job.

As far as foxes, weasels, stoats, mink, rats and various members of the crow family are concerned there is a more permanent option available than simple deterrence. The trap, the snare, the rifle and, in the case of rats, the poisoned bait are all part of the keeper's armoury.

Foxes are controlled by shooting, snaring and, in the spring, by using terriers to kill the cubs in their earths, though at the time of writing it seems likely that government legislation may ban the latter practice. The organised fox drive was once a regular feature on the shooting calendar, usually taking place at the end of the season in February, sometimes combined with the hare shoots that were needed to keep the hare population within check. Nowadays the lamp and the rifle are more commonly used to shoot foxes, and the once abundant hare is given voluntary protection in many parts of the country. Lamping can be extremely effective especially when foxes are squeaked in to rifle range and many keepers enjoy it as a sport in its own right.

It is advisable to inform your local police station when you are going lamping and also to ensure that the farms on the shoot are aware of your activities. Before you start loosing off a centre-fire rifle into the night it is essential that you have a really comprehensive knowledge of the layout of your shoot so that you know where there are houses, roads, rights of way and so on. Never, ever fire at a fox unless you are quite certain that 1) it *is* a fox and not a sheep, badger, pet cat or the like, and 2) that there is a safe backstop for the bullet if you miss, or if it passes right through the fox.

A snare has the advantage of being on duty twenty-four hours a day, though personally I dislike snaring since a fox may be caught in the snare for several hours before being found and humanely destroyed. There is also the danger that you will catch something you weren't intending to trap: dogs, cats, badgers and roe deer are all vulnerable and it is not unknown for sheep and cattle to get a leg snagged in a carelessly set wire. (Putting a stop on the noose so that it cannot tighten fully will largely prevent this.) If you use snares (or any other type of trap) it is a legal requirement that you must inspect them at least once a day, preferably at first light. This can make trapping and snaring difficult for part-time keepers, particularly if they live some distance from the shoot. Snares must also be free-running, the use of self-locking snares having been banned by the Wildlife and Countryside Act 1981 – a statute that sets out much of the legislation applying to the shooting and trapping of pest species.

It is worth making the point that you will never free your shoot of foxes. The saying that 'You kill one fox and two others come to the funeral' is a cliché but it is none the less true for that. If you enjoy lamping and trapping then there is some comfort in this since it means that you are never likely to run out of foxes to hunt.

Gin traps, which worked by catching their victims by the leg, have been banned for many years but there are other, legal traps that may be used to kill stoats and weasels. These are known as break back traps and are designed to snap around the victim's body, literally breaking the back or neck and thus ensuring as far as is possible a quick death for the victim. Often referred to as Fenn traps after one of the manufacturers, they are set in artificial tunnels made of brick, wood, stone or the like and generally rely on the natural curiosity of the stoat and the weasel to draw them into the tunnel, though you can also try to attract them in with a non-poisonous bait. They are particularly useful when set around the perimeter of your release pen to try and stop predators before they get into the pen among your poults. As with snares, they must be inspected at least once every day and are liable to be damaged or destroyed by passing members of the public if they are not well concealed.

Live catch traps, or cage traps are used for mink, baited with fish or cat food and generally set near water courses that mink use as highways. If you catch an otter or a domestic cat in such a trap you can release it unharmed, mink or feral cats should be killed quickly and humanely. Live catch traps are also used for crows and magpies, the

Cage trap for crows with a 'ladder' type entry.

Larsen trap being recognised as a legal device under a general licence issued by the ministry. A Larsen trap is essentially a small crate divided into two compartments with sprung doors giving access to each. Once the first crow or magpie has been caught or scrounged from a neighbouring keeper, it is left in one compartment, with food, water, some form of shelter and enough space to stretch its wings, and hopefully will attract other crows/magpies to the trap.

The Larsen trap has the advantage of being portable and can be moved around the shoot. You can also set up large, fixed cage traps with either ladder or lobster pot type entrances to trap crows and magpies. Again, it is legal to use a live bird as a decoy, provided that it has sufficient space to spread its wings and is provided with food, water and shelter. Space is not generally a problem with the fixed type of cage trap, though passing walkers may be if they feel inclined to open the door and release your decoy and any crows it has attracted to the trap. If you catch any protected species in your cage traps make sure that they are released unharmed. It is not unknown for anti-field sports activists to target keepers by placing a raptor in their cages and hoping to catch them in the act of destroying it.

Rats and mice can be controlled by the use of poison baits where they are a problem, though it is essential that baits are set in such a way that they are inaccessible to anything other than the intended victims. Poison gas such as Cymag can also be used to control rats and rabbits, though it is no longer legal to use it against foxes. Before handling any poison and especially before using Cymag, it is essential to take advice on the proper and safe use of the substance and to abide by the rules and guidelines. You do not want to become a victim yourself.

The amount of predator control that you do will be limited by the time you have available – or are prepared to make available – and by the extent of the problem that predators present. A century ago the principle was much simpler: anything that posed a threat to game was exterminated: but changes in attitude as well as changes in the law mean that a much more reasonable approach must be taken today. Since you may not kill many of the predators that will take your pheasants you have to rely on prevention – scaring them away and designing your release pens to minimise their opportunities to hunt. In some cases it may be simplest to accept that you will lose a proportion of your birds to predation and increase your stocks accordingly.

Security

Security can be quite a contentious issue on a modern shoot. At one time the gamekeepers dispensed their own justice with fists and sticks and in many cases were feared by poachers, often with good cause. The police and the local magistrates could also be relied on to uphold the law with regard to poaching and landowners found it relatively easy to keep the public off their property. Much of that has changed now and the degree of support that a keeper will get from his local police force seems to depend on the area in which he lives. Some forces are excellent and will respond quickly and appropriately to a call for assistance: others seem to regard poaching as a crime that can be largely ignored and believe that the most appropriate response to any incident is to turn up a day or two later and take a statement.

One thing that has changed dramatically is the way in which the courts uphold the 'rights' of the criminal. Where once a keeper could arrest a poacher and march him down to the police station to be charged the odds are that if you did such a thing these days you would find yourself in court accused of assault, false imprisonment, kidnapping and possibly attempted murder. Any keeper becoming involved in a confrontation with poachers or other criminals active in the countryside must be very careful not to get into a situation where he may find himself becoming the subject of criminal proceedings. This is particularly a danger where the keeper is operating alone with only potentially hostile witnesses to his actions.

Pheasant poaching is probably less of a problem than it once was. The value of a dead pheasant is negligible: they may even be unsaleable at some times of the season: and there are far less people living in the countryside with either the knowledge or the desire to get out at night and poach. Larger and more valuable game, particularly deer may attract poachers since there is still money to be made from venison, and illegal hare coursing is a considerable problem in some parts of the country, often carried on quite blatantly in defiance of both keepers and police. If you have problems of this nature it is worth trying to get your local police force involved in some sort of countryside watch scheme. Explaining the real situation to them may help dispense the myth of the 'harmless old poacher taking one for the pot' and could result in a quicker and keener response next time you ask for their help.

Part time keepers are particularly vulnerable to poachers since there is a good chance that their visits to the shoot may be at times proscribed by their day job. If the poacher knows that you will be safely ensconced in your office between nine and five every weekday he can raid your coverts with impunity. Good relations with local people, particularly the farming community can be invaluable to you in this situation. Otherwise, regular and irregular visits to the shoot and a visible presence on the ground will help to deter the casual poacher. Lamping not only helps to keep your foxes under control but the flash of a fox lamp lets the poacher know that you are out and about and may be enough to persuade him that he would be better to take himself elsewhere.

Criminal activity in the countryside is not limited to poaching and illegal coursing. Thefts of farm animals and machinery, particularly things like quad bikes, cause severe problems in many areas. Just being around the shoot and keeping your eyes open provides a useful service to local residents. The development of the mobile phone has made reporting problems and calling for assistance immeasurably easier than it once was. Short-range radios are now legal and cheap to buy and can be useful if you need to coordinate your efforts with others.

The countryside is becoming seen more and more as one big leisure park: an attitude greatly encouraged by the combination of prejudice and ignorance that characterises the government at the time of writing. In many ways the poacher constitutes much less of a threat to the shoot than the thoughtless (or witless) walker who insists on his 'right' to tramp through the middle of your coverts, the 'right' of his dog to run loose among your poults and the 'rights' of his family to break down your fences, leave open your gates and clamber all over valuable farm machinery. Often the best way to counter such trouble is to try and avoid it. Site your release pen as far away

Getting food out to the pheasants in winter is much easier with a quad bike to carry it.

from public footpaths as possible, hide or padlock feed bins, keep traps and snares well out of sight and ensure that snares in particular are checked early in the mornings before the public is out and about.

It can be extremely difficult to stop the idiot who insists on letting his dog run riot. A polite request may be enough with many people but some resolutely refuse to listen to any sort of reasoned argument. An electric fence can be an effective deterrent around the release pen, but it is also easily vandalised. Free-running dogs can sometimes be discouraged by informing their owners that the dog is in danger of getting caught in a fox snare – whether or not you actually have any snares in place –and a notice warning of the presence of snakes can also have the desired effect. As with the snares, no actual snakes are required.

Shoot Day Management

A driven shoot day may involve anything from a dozen to fifty people. There are the guns, obviously, and the beaters to provide them with some pheasants to shoot at, as an absolute minimum. Then there may be pickers-up, loaders, stops and flankers, perhaps a second team of beaters blanking in birds to one wood while another is being driven, drivers for the game cart, beaters' wagon and guns' transport and possibly catering staff. All these people have to be controlled and coordinated, and on many shoots the job of controlling and coordinating falls squarely onto the shoulders of the keeper.

Arrangements vary greatly from shoot to shoot. In some cases the keeper is primarily in charge of the beaters: in others he is expected to position the guns, liase with the pickers-up, brace and hang shot pheasants, drive one of the wagons and generally oversee everything except (and sometimes even including) lunch. And run the beating line as well, of course. Shoot day management can be stressful to say the least. How stressful will depend to a large extent on how familiar your guns and beaters are with the way the shoot is run. If the guns have all been syndicate members for many years and the beaters your regular crew for the past several seasons things can seem, at times, to pretty much run themselves. If you have a party of visiting guns, a scratch team of beaters, most of whom have never seen the shoot before, and a distinct dearth of picking up dogs then you are likely to spend the entire day chasing your tail. That's shooting for you.

In an ideal world there would be little need for an organiser on shoot days. The guns would go quietly and quickly to their pegs, the beaters would keep a straight line as they worked through the coverts and all the dogs would be paragons of virtue. In the real world things don't happen quite like that.

It is a fact of life that any enterprise involving more than two or three people acting towards a common purpose will run smoothly only if there is someone nominally in charge to organise the work and tell the others what to do. The majority of people will be much happier if they are given clear instructions in the role they are to play than if they are left to find their own place in the general scheme of things. It doesn't matter whether they are a gun or a beater, they will be more confident and do a better job if they know what they are supposed to be doing, where they are meant to stand, which

Always draw for positions: it saves a lot of hassle later.

part of the wood they should be working their dog through, where to go at the end of the drive, whether to stay behind and hunt for that lost pheasant or move off and leave it to the picker up.

I have been on one or two shoots where no one was in charge (or was prepared to assume the role of shoot captain) and they simply didn't work. Lots of time was spent standing around while tentative suggestions were advanced as to where we might go next: the beaters tended to wander through the woods in twos and threes, gossiping instead of concentrating on finding pheasants, and the guns spent an age deciding where each of them was going to stand.

Quite often these kind of problems stem from an excess of politeness. When we are working the pointers on the hill there are usually half a dozen guns out and the arrangement is that two guns will come forward each time a dog points grouse. There is nothing more frustrating for a dog handler than standing waiting interminably, knowing that the grouse are flighty and probably about to rise at any moment, while the guns stand around a hundred yards away and argue about who should go to the point.

Note that these arguments always – and I do mean *always* – arise because the guns are trying to give the other guns the best of the sport. I have never heard anyone say 'It's *my* turn!' The argument is always: 'You go this time.' 'No, no: I've had more shooting than you: you go.' 'I went to the last point.' 'Yes, but you didn't get a shot....' I know that the guns are being polite and considerate, that they are trying to ensure

Checking with the guns at the end of the drive to see how many birds are to be picked.

that their friends get the most out of their day on the hill, but believe me: when you are standing waiting… And waiting… And the grouse are sticking their heads up above the heather ready to fly… Trust me: politeness is fine, but things run a lot better when someone seizes the day by the scruff of its neck, says 'Fred and John: it's your turn', sends them on their way and brooks no nonsense from anyone. We shoot a lot more grouse that way too.

I am not arguing that some kind of martinet is required, bellowing orders from dawn to dusk and browbeating everybody into following some master plan. It is simply that people work better, individually and as a group, when they know what they are supposed to be doing, and know that someone, somewhere is 'in charge' and responsible for what is happening. Indeed, I think it is the question of responsibility that makes the difference between organisation and chaos.

Suppose you are one of half a dozen beaters about to work through a wood. There is a relatively open part at the top of the wood with beech trees and odd scraps of bramble for cover while down below is a tangle of thick undergrowth. Are you going to be flogging your way through the thick stuff or ambling along in the relatively open ground at the top of the hill? If you are at the top will you feel guilty at dodging the worst of the work? If you are at the bottom will you be resentful of the slackers up in the open ground? Perhaps you'll wander along on the edge of the thick stuff 'letting the dog do the work' while you have a natter with the other four beaters who are doing the same thing.

How much better things will work if someone has come along right at the start and given everyone clear instructions. 'A, B and C: would you work your dogs along at the top of the wood and keep a bit ahead of the line to try and stop birds breaking out on the right? D, you haven't got a dog so would you go forward and tap the fence by the gate to stop the pheasants running out and into the turnips? The rest of you come with me and we'll work through the thick stuff. Give your dogs plenty of time because the pheasants will be sitting tight.' Now everyone knows where to go and what to do. They can get on with their job and not worry about whether they are doing the right thing or if they should be in a different spot altogether. If things don't go quite right: if a lot of birds break back away from the guns or if the pheasants are trying to run out along one of the hedges: then there is someone in charge to try and sort it out: to hold the line while another stop goes forward or to send the walking gun back to take advantage of those escaping birds. The important thing is that *someone* is in charge and everyone else knows who he is and where to look for instructions or changes to the plan.

Exactly how you give your instructions is really a matter of individual management style, which is a fancy way of saying that different people have different personalities and thus different ways of getting things done. Some keepers run their beating line with military precision. Some seem to think the only way to get beaters to work properly is to scream abuse at them from the start of the drive to the finish. Others adopt a much softer approach, quietly letting the things happen and only getting involved if something has to be changed. There are keepers who always put themselves through the thickest and hardest of the cover and there are keepers who ensure that they never personally get near a thorn or a bramble. Everyone is different and everyone has their own ideas as to where they will be most useful.

How you run your beating line depends on your own attitude and that of the beaters who make up your team. Some people can be led: others may have to be driven. Some accept responsibility: others dodge it at every turn. If you are in charge then it is up to you to work out how to get the best from your beaters, both as a team and as individuals. Having worked as a beater for quite a lot of different keepers as well as trying to run a beating line myself on numerous occasions I pretty much know what works for me whether I am in charge or in harness as it were. I hope the following will be of some help to you.

1. Make sure that everyone knows what they are trying to do. It may be that the covert is absolutely straight forward: just start at one end and work through to the other, but it is still worth saying so at the beginning. If the drive is going to involve a certain amount of pivoting and turning, of holding back one end of the line while the other end blanks in a spur of the wood, then make sure that everyone knows what is expected of them before you start. You may know that the plan is to hold the left of the line while the right swings round above them, but if all your beaters have heard is a single cry of 'Hold the left!' they are going to be standing about wondering whether they should start forward again because they can hear the other half of the line pressing on. All it takes is someone to use their initiative and say 'I reckon we'd better push along.' and suddenly your master plan is ruined. So make sure everyone knows what's happening, don't keep it all to yourself.

If you can't be there yourself put one of the beaters in charge at the start of the drive.

2.A little bit of personal attention – call it flattery if you like – helps. The best keeper I have ever known for running a beating line always made a point of having a quick word with each of the beaters, telling him what he wanted them to do – even if it was only to go and tap the fence at the end of the wood. He always sent you off feeling that you were playing an important part in the plan and that he had picked you – you personally – as the right man to do that job. In truth it might be that you were being sent to 'Work along the hedge and bring it down to the top corner of the wood, then stay there are tap to stop the birds running back up' because that was one way of keeping you and your wild dog as far away from the pheasants as possible, but that wasn't the impression you got. You were always left with the notion that a) there was a plan, and b) you had a vital part to play in its success.

3.Try and strike a balance between giving no orders and giving too many orders. Even when things are running perfectly (if there ever is such a day) it may not be a bad idea to hold the line perhaps just once or twice during a drive so as to remind everyone that you are there and keeping an eye on things and that there is some sort of control in place. That said, please don't fall into the habit of constantly starting and stopping the beating line; endlessly holding the left, or the right, or the centre; sending the dogs on or calling the dogs in; niggling and nagging and getting on everybody's nerves because they know that there is absolutely no need for all the starting, stopping and turning around beyond the desire to meddle and perhaps to hear their own voice. All that happens, in the end, is that no one listens any more.

It is always best to ensure that someone is in charge and that everyone else knows it.

4.A little bit of praise and a word of thanks will always go down well. If the drive has gone well then say well done to the beating team. Everyone likes to be told they are doing a good job. Most people like it even better when you tell them that their dog is doing a good job. Always make a point of thanking your beaters at the end of the day. It doesn't cost anything but it does make a difference.

5.Try to even out the work among the team. Okay: you may have to keep putting one or two of the beaters into the thickest parts of the cover simply because they are the only ones with dogs willing and able to get in there and flush the pheasants, but if that is the case then make sure they know how much you appreciate it. Otherwise, switch things around so that everyone gets a turn at going to the top of the hill, or forcing their way through the thick stuff, and everyone gets their fair share of the easier bits.

6.Please mind your language. You are going to have to shout quite loudly at times particularly when the beating line is spread out across a wide covert. Remember that it isn't only the beaters that can hear you. There may be ladies present with the guns: indeed, some of the guns may be ladies: and you never know who else might be within earshot. A stream of bad language emanating from the woods at a hundred and twenty decibels does nothing for the good image of shooting and countrysports in general.

7.Finally, and perhaps most importantly, try to make the work of the beating line as enjoyable as possible. I realise that may be a tall order on a cold, wet, miserable January day when the trees are dripping slush down your necks and everyone is just longing for the whistle that will signal the end of the final drive, but try nevertheless. Most of your team are likely to be there from choice rather than economic necessity and if the job starts to become a drudge instead of fun they are likely to stop coming. A bit of a laugh and a joke, the odd word of praise and a genuine thank-you at the end of the day cost nothing and will be appreciated by nearly everybody.

Pickers-up are a slightly different breed to beaters in that they tend to work much more on their own initiative. Some of the bigger shoots have a whole team of pickers-up working under the guidance of a keeper or team captain, while smaller shoots may struggle to spare anyone from the beating line in order to pick up. As with beaters, the main thing to ensure with your pickers-up is that they have a clear idea of what they are supposed to be doing.

The basics of the job are simple enough. Stand well back behind the guns, ideally where they have a clear view of the action, and watch where the pheasants fall with particular attention to pricked birds and runners that may have to be collected quickly if they are to be collected at all. Make certain though that you let your pickers-up know *before* the drive if you don't want them to send their dogs into one of the other coverts because it will be shot later. It's no good assuming that they will know, or guess correctly at, your plan for the rest of the day.

Ideally, at the end of the drive you should check with the guns to find out how many birds are to be picked, and from where, and then tally up with the pickers-up to see how many are still left to gather. You need fairly precise information at this point: not just of the number of pheasants shot but as exact details as possible of where they fell. It helps if you know your guns: that is to say, know those who have a realistic idea of the number of birds they have killed and those who are prone to claim several 'hard-hit and probably lying dead' from among their clean misses. Then you can organise one or two of the pickers-up to stay behind if necessary and catch up after the next drive so that any missing birds can be picked without holding up the whole shoot.

Obviously, if you are leaving anyone behind it is important that they know where to find you when they have collected the last of the pheasants, and that they have some means of getting there. If your drives are spread out over several square miles of countryside your team are going to need either local knowledge or a good map, plus clear instructions, if *you* are not going to end up searching for the *them*.

Getting a clear picture of the total number of pheasants shot gets more difficult as the numbers increase. If a gun has only shot two or three birds during the drive there is no excuse for him not knowing where they fell, but on a big shoot, where each gun may have fired a couple of boxes of cartridges, killed twenty or thirty pheasants and at times have been rushing to get the gun reloaded as the next bunch of birds sailed overhead, it is understandable if they are a little bit vague as to exactly where every pheasant landed. Hopefully, if you are shooting those sort of numbers, you will have a good team of experienced pickers-up to assist you otherwise you can only guess and hope.

If the guns are regulars they should know where to stand without the need for guidance.

The guns themselves have to be organised as well as the supporting staff. This may be the job of the host, or of the shoot captain, but it is not unusual for the keeper to have to sort this part of the day out as well as the beaters and pickers-up. Arrangements vary from shoot to shoot, and if you are lucky you may have someone reliable to run the beating line leaving you free to work with the guns, but it is quite possible that you will have to do both jobs. The first problem then is how you are going to be in two places at once. A lot depends on the layout of the shoot and how far it is from the where the guns stand to where the beaters begin the drive. If the distance is considerable you may have to deputise either one of the guns or one of the beaters to take charge in your absence, at least for the first part of the drive.

An experienced keeper once told me that guns were like dogs and wives: they needed handling politely but firmly with no nonsense being tolerated under any circumstances. While I certainly wouldn't subscribe completely to this doctrine there is certainly a grain of truth as far as dogs and guns are concerned. They may well be paying – perhaps quite a lot of money – for their day shooting, but they still have to obey the shoot rules. A polite but firm approach is usually the best way of ensuring that this happens.

Never leave it to the guns to sort out among themselves who will stand where at each drive. Draw for places. It doesn't matter whether you number from the left or the right; whether you move up two or down three between drives or whether you have some immensely complicated method of even numbers moving up two while odd numbers move down three until lunch and then swap over, except when we do the snipe bog and revert to our original numbers. Draw for places to start with. That way you avoid arguments, accusations of favouritism and those endless discussions between drives.

Most guns, in my experience, are only too anxious to ensure that everyone gets their fair share of the day's sport. Occasionally you will come across what I have heard called a 'hungry' gun: someone who wants all the best shooting for himself and will do his utmost to try to ensure that he gets it. We are all familiar with the sort of thing that can go on if it is not checked and checked firmly as soon as it starts. There is the 'slight adjustment to where the guns stand' ploy. This involves edging the guns along or squeezing the spacing between guns up until Mr Hungry is standing in the prime slot. Then there is the 'double guns' scenario. Mr Hungry leaves his own peg and goes round to stand behind the guns in the centre of the line. This can be 'justified' by claiming that there were lots of birds not being shot at (or missed) by the guns standing at numbers four and five coupled to a (usually spurious) claim that 'we need to get the numbers up'. There are various other ploys but they all have one thing in common. They need to be stamped on – politely but firmly of course – but stamped on nonetheless. Otherwise you will end up with anarchy among your guns.

The best way to keep control of the guns is to have a draw for places and then ensure – politely but firmly – that the guns stand in the places they have drawn *and stay there*. There may be exceptions to this rule: the guns at either end of the line for example may be given the option of starting out walking with the beating line, or allowed to adjust their position depending on whether birds are flying back along the edges of the wood: but in general, if the guns are told where their peg is and given to

A happy gun at the end of the drive is what keepering is all about.

understand that they are expected to stay there, far less problems will arise than if they are allowed to use their initiative and wander about. And it helps considerably if you have numbered markers to show them exactly where to stand.

Keeping things moving between drives is also an important part of managing the guns. Winter days are short enough without wasting a lot of time coffee-housing after each drive. There is a need to strike a sensible balance here. The guns should not feel that they are being harried from one stand to the next without time for a little socialising, a nip from the flask or a swig of coffee, but neither should the whole shoot be delayed because one or two guns want to spend half an hour discussing stock market movements, the cost of a new Bentley or the latest trends in house prices. Keep things moving along and ensure that you get the planned number of drives in before the daylight vanishes. Believe me: the guns who muttered most about being asked to hurry along will be the very ones who complain loudest if the final drive of the day has to be cancelled because the light has gone.

One problem that may arise is what to do if one of the guns starts shooting low birds or worse, fires a dangerous shot. Deciding how to deal with this sort of situation is never easy and will depend to some extent on the person involved: whether the problem is caused by inexperience, carelessness or blind stupidity and whether they will react best to a quiet word or a public dressing down. Sometimes the best solution is to gather all the guns round and draw their attention to the problem without singling out the guilty party: in another case it might be better to speak privately with the person involved. In an extreme case, especially if perhaps alcohol was involved and you felt there was a possibility of another dangerous shot being fired, you might even have to ban the gun from shooting. Whatever action you take it is nearly always best to take it quickly while the memory of the incident is still fresh in everyone's minds.

Shoot day management doesn't end just because the last drive is over. The game has to be sorted out and hung in the larder or divided between the guns depending on the arrangements your particular shoot has for its disposal. Most guns like to know the total bag for the day: not just pheasants, but woodcock, pigeons, partridges, duck and whatever else may have featured: even crows and foxes. The beaters have to be paid or given a brace of birds apiece, arrangements may have to made for the next shoot day and there may still be birds to pick that have eluded everyone during the course of the day. Then there are the dogs to feed, perhaps some guns to clean, the game book to update and the game dealer to contact before you can finally sink into that hot bath – and start thinking about what you have to do tomorrow.

That's keepering for you.

10

AND FINALLY...

Reading back over the previous nine chapters it seems to me that I have asked a lot of questions yet provided very few straight answers and that, I must confess, is pretty much what pheasant shooting is all about. Indeed, a great deal of the attraction of pheasant shooting is precisely that it can offer so much variety to the aspiring sportsman.

You can shoot pheasants that have been driven from a steep-sided, thickly-wooded valley in Devon or walked up on a flat fen in Lincolnshire. You can shoot them as they fly out of a hanging beech wood on the side of the downs or a dark forestry plantation above a salmon river in the Highlands: from a bracken-covered bank on a remote farm in the Welsh hills or from among centuries-old oak trees in an ancient forest in the heart of England. You can, if the fancy takes you, travel all over the world to test your marksmanship against this brightly feathered exile from the Far East. The pheasant may have started its travels in the jungles of China, India and Malaya, but now it is established all around the globe and looks set to stay.

There are shoots that can guarantee to show you enough birds for a decent team of guns to shoot a thousand pheasants in a day, and there are shoots where half a dozen birds in the bag will represent a minor triumph for the men and dogs taking part. There are big, commercial shoots that release poults by the thousand and tiny rough shoots where the only pheasants are those that live wild among the woods and hedgerows. You may be invited to shoot pheasants just once a year on a keeper's day as a reward for a dozen or twenty days spent beating so that others may shoot. You could, if you had the time, the money and the inclination, arrange to shoot pheasants six days a week, every week, from the 1st of October to the 1st of February – though unless it fell on a Sunday and was already discounted you would also have to miss out Christmas Day. I daresay it wouldn't be too much of a wrench.

With so much variety on offer it is hardly surprising that there are no simple answers to many of the questions that a novice to pheasant shooting might pose. The best gun to buy? It might be a simple, plain boxlock picked up second-hand for under a hundred pounds, or it might be a custom built best English sidelock, self-opening ejector, delivered only after a two-year wait and at a cost that would purchase a substantial house in some parts of the country. The right clothes to wear? Army surplus camouflage gear or bespoke tailored tweed suits: an old pair of wellies or leather boots hand-stitched on your own last? Where to shoot? A mooch around the hedgerows on a local farm or the exclusive coverts of a great estate. You choose.

Waiting for a shot on a sunny autumn afternoon.

One of the reasons why there is such a wide choice of pheasant shooting is that it is all, in a sense, artificial sport. The pheasant is not a native of Britain, though having been in residence for something like two thousand years I suppose it must be close to becoming naturalised. But where grouse and partridge, wood pigeon and wildfowl, snipe and woodcock all live here under the conditions of their choice, the pheasant lives, to a great extent, in those places where man decides it should live. True, partridges and mallard are also reared and released in much the same way as pheasants, but in these cases the aim is to supplement the wild birds that are there (or were once there) naturally. And I will grant that the red-legged partridge is also an in-comer, though one that already had family resident here in the form of the grey partridge. But the pheasant was brought here as a complete stranger and as such has been forced to adapt to an alien climate, landscape and diet.

It is this ability to adapt that has made the pheasant into our most common game bird. Where grouse, snipe, woodcock and wildfowl will only thrive where conditions are right, the pheasant will adapt his lifestyle to suit the local habitat – within reason. When this willingness to adapt is combined with man's ability to mould the countryside in order provide suitable habitat for pheasants it is easy to see why pheasant shooting has become such a popular and widespread sport.

Precisely because pheasant shoots are artificial and because we can control the level of sport so precisely there is a danger that we may start to take our pheasant shooting too much for granted. Shooting has come a long way since the first huntsmen set out with their clumsy and unreliable weapons to bring some meat to the table. We must never regard the pheasant, or any other game bird for that matter, as no more than a target to test our marksmanship or a statistic to be boasted about at the end of the drive. Pheasant shooting as a sport may be something that man has contrived rather than the harvesting of a natural resource, but no matter how artificial the environment, pheasant shooting is still, essentially, a matter of man exercising his natural instinct to hunt in order to put food on his table. If we forget that then we risk treating the pheasant with no more respect than we would afford to a clay pigeon.

And beyond question the pheasant is worth much more than that. It is a long, long time since I shot my first pheasant in that frozen sprout field under a grey Suffolk sky, but I can still remember the delight I felt at holding and admiring him: that gorgeous, gaudy plumage, the iridescent sheen of the head, the pure white neck ring and the fact that he was *my* pheasant. No pheasant since then has ever come near to matching the thrill of shooting my first pheasant, but I still try to recapture a little of the delight and awe that I felt then whenever I go pheasant shooting, and always to treat the quarry with respect. We are, after all, sportsmen, and being a sportsman involves a lot more than just killing pheasants.

In common with all our fieldsports pheasant shooting is in danger of being banned in accordance with the demands of a small but vociferous minority acting on the ignorance and prejudice of some of our members of parliament. The Scottish Parliament (a grand name for what is no more than an extra level of local government) has already introduced legislation that purports to ban hunting, (though its main effect has been to increase the number of foxes killed by hunts) and it looks likely that the Westminster legislators will soon try to do something similar. Once hunting is banned

A wintry morning and a good shot at a driven pheasant.

there is no doubt that shooting will be the next target, possibly through a ban on rearing and releasing game birds or via ever more swingeing restrictions on gun ownership.

But for the moment we are still free to enjoy our traditional country pastimes of which pheasant shooting is perhaps the most democratic, appealing to, and available to, the widest possible range of sportsmen. From the rough shooter enjoying a lonely walk with just a spaniel for company and no higher expectation than that he might go home with his dinner in the game bag to the grandest of driven shoots: from the beater with dog and stick to the gun with his matched pair of Purdeys: pheasant shooting has something to offer everyone who enjoys country sports.

Let us hope that it will be allowed to do so for many years to come.

Ready for action at a Cocker Spaniel Field Trial.

SHOOTING ORGANISATIONS

Everyone who takes part in pheasant shooting, whether as a gun, a beater, a picker-up, a gamekeeper or a shoot manager will be aware of the pressure being brought to bear on all fieldsports: pressure that could easily result in shooting being banned completely or so bound in by restrictions as to become impractical for most people. There are a number of organisations devoted to defending shooting, looking after the interests of the countryside community and carrying out research into game management. Several also provide third-party insurance for their members. Everyone who shoots or supports shooting should be a member of at least one.

Everyone who enjoys shooting should support the organisations that exist to defend our right to take part.

The Countryside Alliance

The Countryside Alliance is the primary focus for the defence of all fieldsports against those who threaten them on political or moral grounds.

Address: The Countryside Alliance, The Old Town Hall, 367 Kennington Road, London, SE11 4PT Telephone 0207 840 9274 Website www.countryside-alliance.com.

British Association for Shooting and Conservation (BASC)

BASC was formed from the old Wildfowlers Association of Great Britain and Ireland (WAGBI). It campaigns against political interference in shooting and also runs conservation and research programmes as well as providing third-party insurance for its members.

Address: BASC, Marford Mill, Rossett, Wrexham, Clywd LL12 0HL. Telephone 01244 573000 Website www.basc.org.uk

The Game Conservancy Trust

The Game Conservancy is a charitable trust and thus precluded from the political campaigning that the other shooting organisations carry out. It is deeply involved in research into all aspects of game and countryside management and conservation and provides a valuable advisory service to its members.

Address: The Game Conservancy Trust, Fordingbridge, Hampshire SP6 1EF. Telephone 01425 652381 Website www.gct.org.uk

The National Gamekeepers Organisation (NGO)

The NGO promotes the work of gamekeepers, supports and defends the work of both professional and amateur keepers and campaigns on behalf of shooting and fieldsports in general.

Address: NGO, PO Box 107, Bishop Auckland, DL14 9YW Telephone 01388 718502 Website www.nationalgamekeepers.org.uk

The Scottish Gamekeepers Association (SGA)

The SGA is the Scottish equivalent of the NGO.

Address: The Scottish Gamekeepers Association, PO Box 7477, Perth, Perthshire PH2 7YE Telephone 01738 587515 Website www.scottishgamekeepers.co.uk

INDEX